create jewelry

crystals

create **jewelry**
crystals

Marlene Blessing and Jamie Hogsett | Editors of *Beadwork* magazine

INTERWEAVE PRESS
interweave.com

ACKNOWLEDGMENTS

We give our most heartfelt thanks to Swarovski International, Inc., whose support greatly enriched our exploration of crystal jewelry designs. Special thanks go to some key people at the company who welcomed our questions, fed our enthusiasm for crystals, and gave us encouragement from beginning to end: Stefan Elschwiger, Dr. Elisabeth Azwanger, Katharina Kuen, Heike Baschta, Verena Koetzle, and Cynthia Pino. Rebecca Whittaker, DIY Segment Manager for Swarovski North America, offered her generous assistance at every turn, including coordinating the contribution of the Swarovski crystals that are used in all of the projects within. Special thanks to Betcey, Mark, and Star of Beyond Beadery for opening their home and assisting with the selection of seed beads for all of the projects.

For my niece Melanie, who shines with beauty and intelligence. —MB

For my mom, Gail Kanemoto Hogsett, who aways sparkles. —JH

All designs and instructions, Jamie Hogsett. All narrative text, Marlene Blessing.

Photography, Joe Coca (unless otherwise specified)

Interweave Press LLC
201 East Fourth Street
Loveland, Colorado 80537 USA
interweave.com

Printed in China by Asia Pacific.

Library of Congress Cataloging-in-Publication Data

Blessing, Marlene, 1947-
  Creating jewelry : crystals, dazzling designs to make and wear / Marlene Blessing and Jamie Hogsett, authors.
     p. cm.
  Includes bibliographical references and index.
  ISBN 978-1-59668-022-7 (pbk. : alk. paper)
  1. Beadwork. 2. Jewelry making. 3. Crystals. I. Hogsett, Jamie, 1978- II. Title.
  TT860.B649 2007
  739.27--dc22

                                      2007008915

10 9 8 7 6 5 4 3 2 1

The Allure of Light   6

The Many Facets of Crystal   7

The Allure of Light

A Radiant Favorite

CRYSTALS ARE A SHINING FAVORITE AMONG JEWELRY designers, bead artists, and anyone who can appreciate the radiant beauty of these precious givers of light. Crystals can flash with fiery heat, cast a warm, persistent glow, or make a bold statement with their icy elegance.

No matter what their effect in a jewelry design, crystals captivate us with their gemlike sparkle. Like gems, crystals have played—and continue to play—their part in adorning us. In the Roaring Twenties, flappers achieved razzle-dazzle as they danced with abandon in short dresses dripping with crystal embellishments. Today, wedding dresses, hair pieces, and jewelry are often sprinkled with crystals, illuminating a unique brilliance on a most special day. For celebrities parading their glamorous selves at a red carpet awards ceremony, crystals adorn countless designer gowns, handbags, shoes, and other accessories. These faceted wonders cast a spell on us that is impossible to shake. Is it any surprise that we are entranced by their shimmering delights and want to showcase them in our handmade jewelry?

As you explore the jewelry and the crystal lore in the pages to come, you will find dazzling designs that fit many moods and occasions. You will also learn some fascinating stories along the way, stories that describe the qualities and powers of both natural rock crystal and the many-hued man-made crystals available everywhere. Choose a Classic piece, such as a bracelet of roughly faceted rock crystals or a necklace with Art Nouveau spirit, to express your appreciation of the past. Or find a necklace richly studded with showy asymmetrical topaz crystals to fit your Special-Occasion needs. And for the times when you want to make a Fashion-Forward statement, pick a trio of brightly woven crystal bangles in Caribbean hues. Whatever your style, whatever your creative impulse, dive into the glittering possibilities ahead. As you savor an array of original projects, accompanied by clear instructions and stunning photography, we know you will continue to be inspired to create your own crystal keepsakes.

the many facets of
crystal

Form and Substance

Every mineral on earth is formed of crystals that combine in unique three-dimensional patterns. What we call rock crystal is a pure form of quartz, completely without coloration and composed of silicon dioxide, or silica (SiO_2). Rock crystal is found in deposits around the world and was used through the centuries as a gemstone for ornamentation and as a substance from which various religious and utilitarian objects were carved. The stone's waterlike clarity, its relative hardness (7 on the Mohs Scale of Hardness—a scale of mineral hardness created by German mineralogist, Friedrich Mohs—compared to a 10 for diamonds), and its abundance made it very desirable to early makers of jewelry and their clients.

Quartz crystal

Popular Crystal Shapes*

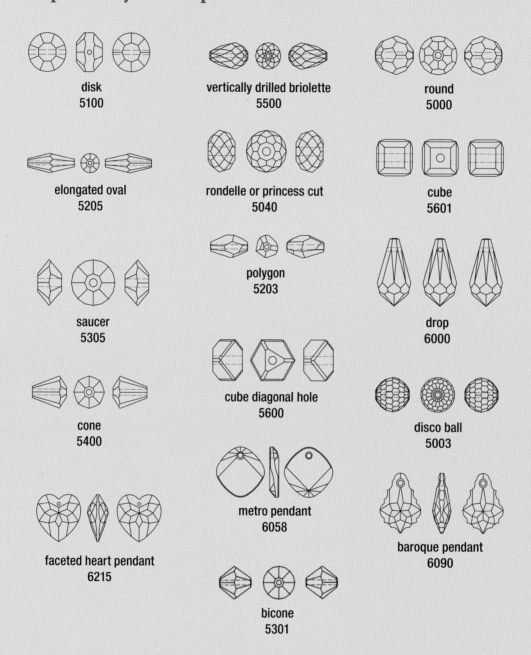

disk
5100

vertically drilled briolette
5500

round
5000

elongated oval
5205

rondelle or princess cut
5040

cube
5601

saucer
5305

polygon
5203

drop
6000

cone
5400

cube diagonal hole
5600

disco ball
5003

faceted heart pendant
6215

metro pendant
6058

baroque pendant
6090

bicone
5301

* These shape numbers correspond to the numbers in each project's materials list. Please note that not all shapes are included on this chart.

Courtesy of Swarovski.

Glass Becomes Crystal

With a stone as popular as rock crystal, it was perhaps inevitable that once a man-made version of it could be produced reliably, artisans would embrace the innovation. Although leaded glass was invented at the end of the seventeenth century, it was not until the eighteenth century that techniques for producing completely transparent leaded glass were perfected. The formula involved combining silica (sand quartz), lime, and soda or ash—with lead added to brighten and intensify the colors and clarity. Proud of their achievement, European glassmakers began to advertise their crystal-clear products, and ultimately the term "crystal" came to apply to the glass.

Crystals—An Essential for Designing Beaders

While natural rock crystal beads are available for our jewelry designs today, they are not as plentiful or varied as glass crystal beads. And rock crystals are usually much more expensive. To honor the stone that inspired the creation of the man-made crystal, we've sprinkled intriguing bits of lore and history about rock crystals throughout this book. And we've even included a couple of jewelry designs with significant rock crystal beauty. The majority of the dazzling designs within, however, feature manufactured crystals in all of their diverse splendor. No matter whose bead trend surveys you might read, those who love to make their own beaded jewelry always rank crystals at the top of their must-have list.

Courtesy of Swarovski

This Swarovski crystal figurine, entitled "Ray," is 9 ⅝ × 6 ½ inches and embodies the beauty and elegance of faceted crystal.

Courtesy of Swarovski

Crystal Colors and Effects
(Underline indicates an exclusive color)

Colors

 Crystal
001

 Black Diamond
215

 Light Azore
361

 Aquamarine
202

 Light Sapphire
211

 Indian Sapphire
217

 Sapphire
206

 Capri Blue
243

 Montana
207

 Chrysolite
238

 Peridot
214

 Erinite
360

 Indicolite
379

 Blue Zircon
229

 Emerald
205

 Jonquil
213

 Light Topaz
226

 Khaki
550

 Lime
385

 Olivine
228

 Fireopal
237

 Padparadscha
542

 Hyacinth
236

 Indian Red
374

 Light Siam
227

 Siam
208

 Ruby
501

 Garnet
241

 Burgundy
515

 Silk
391

 Light Peach
362

 Light Colorado Topaz
246

 Topaz
203

 Light Smoked Topaz
221

 Smoked Topaz
220

 Smoky Quartz
225

 Light Rose
223

 Rose
209

 Fuchsia
502

 Amethyst
204

 Light Amethyst
212

 Violet
371

 Tanzanite
539

 Purple Velvet
277

 White Opal
234

 Pacific Opal
390

Caribbean Blue Opal
394

Violet Opal
389

White Alabaster
281

Jet
280

Turquoise
267

Rose Alabaster
293

Effects

 Crystal
Aurore Boreale
001 AB

 Crystal
Aurore Boreale 2x
001 AB2

 Crystal Satin
001 SAT

 Crystal Comet
Argent Light
001 CAL

 Crystal Matt Finish
001 MAT

 White Opal Sky Blue
234 SBL

 White Opal
Star Shine
234 STS

 Crystal
Bermuda Blue
001 BBL

Crystal Heliotrope
001 HEL

 Crystal Metallic
Blue 2x
001 METB2

 Crystal Silver Shade
001 SSHA

 Crystal
Golden Shadow
001 GSHA

Crystal Copper
001 COP

Crystal Dorado 2x
001 DOR2

Jet Hematite
280 HEM

Jet Hematite 2x
280 HEM2

Jet Nut 2x
280 NUT2

Crystal Vitrail
Medium
001 VM

Separate and Not Equal

Rhinestones, paste, and crystals are not one in the same—although many use these designations simultaneously. Nor were they developed to be "diamond pretenders" or "fabulous fakes"—although the best of them can certainly do the job.

High-quality natural rock crystals sifted from the Rhine River were called rhinestones and were cut and faceted to create jewelry worthy of a royal. However, over time, the name has come to refer to faceted lead crystal or faceted glass, usually backed with foil. The predecessors of today's glass mass-produced rhinestone "bling" were highly valued and handcrafted by the most skilled artisans of the time.

Paste refers to glass with very high lead content, which was originally faceted to be incorporated in the jewelry, buckles, and other items of adornment worn by fashionable eighteenth-century ladies and gentlemen. Once cut by a master craftsman, the stones were coated with a metal coating or foiling to add brilliance and enhance the refractions of light. Ironically, because paste could be more easily cut and shaped than diamonds, the craftsman who worked with paste often had greater gem-cutting skills than those who worked with precious diamonds. Such was the high quality of paste jewelry that even the ill-fated French queen, Marie Antoinette, owned many pieces.

Today's premier crystal manufacturer, Swarovski, produces more than 100,000 different shapes, colors, sizes, and facets of crystals. Their glass crystals are made from a carefully protected formula (glass with a certain percentage of lead) and are precision cut by the company's unequaled machinery, first developed in 1892. Swarovski has also created unique coatings or "effects" for its crystals. The first and most well known of these was the Aurora Borealis or AB coating that the company developed in concert with fashion designer Christian Dior in the mid-1950s. This distinctive finish, still applied to many of the company's crystals, adds an opalescent glow.

Glamorous film legend Marlene Dietrich often wore spectacular jewelry that incorporated crystals instead of precious gems.

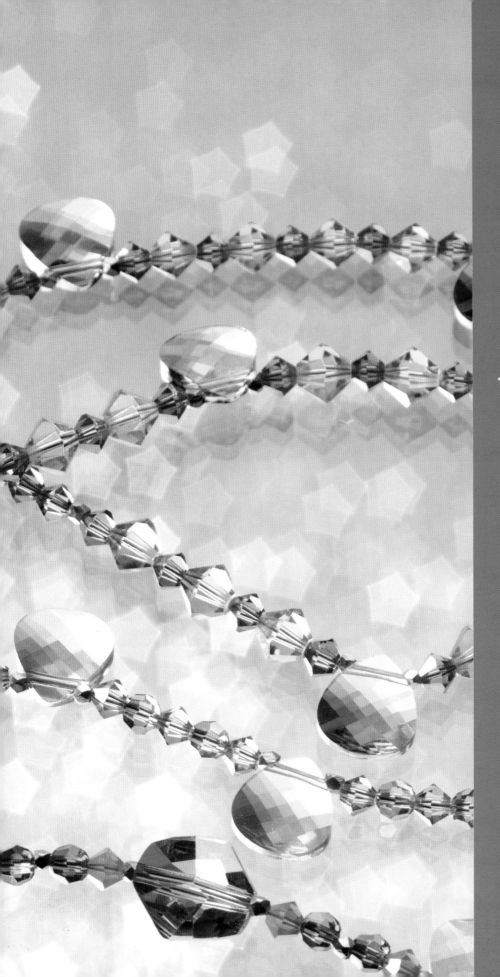

the
projects

classic

Green fir swags are fragrant, lining your fireplace mantel and draping the railing on your staircase. Candles have been lit, soft holiday music is playing, and you have filled small bowls throughout the house with spicy potpourri. All is in festive order. The darkness outside contrasts sharply with the twinkling lights in your home.

Having slipped on your classic little black dress for this occasion, it's time to choose a signature bracelet, necklace, or earrings that make you feel like the fabulous hostess you are. And what will make this an even sweeter choice is that you've made your own stylish jewelry from dazzling crystals.

You've planned this annual gathering for weeks, making sure all the finishing touches signal warm celebration. The rituals of baking, of preparing special hors d'oeuvres, and of making pomegranate-orange punch are something you look forward to with happy anticipation. For special effect, you have made a stylish centerpiece for the dining table—a spray of gauzy ribbons with tiny blown-glass ornaments and brass bells tied to them.

In a setting infused with light, you are radiant. Perhaps you've decided on the multistrand necklace of midnight-dark crystals, which feels cool and opulent against your neck. Or maybe the earrings with bright, dangling crystal stars send the very message you most desire: May your New Year be bright!

Arabian Nights

MATERIALS

176 dark purple opaque luster size 15° seed beads

166 purple galvanized size 11° seed beads

104 grape matte lined size 11° seed beads

8 grape lined size 8° seed beads

24 purple velvet 4mm crystal rounds (5000)

24 purple velvet 4mm crystal helix beads

32 purple velvet 4mm crystal bicones (5301)

49 crystal comet argent light 4mm crystal bicones (5301)

24 purple velvet 6mm crystal rounds (5000)

25 purple velvet 6mm crystal helix beads

36 purple velvet 6mm crystal rondelles (5040)

32 purple velvet 6mm crystal bicones (5301)

43 crystal comet argent light 6mm crystal bicones (5301)

18 purple velvet 6mm crystal cubes (5601)

12 purple velvet 8mm crystal rounds (5000)

12 purple velvet 8mm crystal helix beads

25 purple velvet 8mm crystal rondelles (5040)

24 purple velvet 8mm crystal cubes (5601)

1 sterling silver 25mm toggle clasp

10 sterling silver 2mm crimp tubes

4" (10cm) of sterling silver 22-gauge wire

120" (305cm) of .019 beading wire

TOOLS

Wire cutters

Flat-nose pliers

Round-nose pliers

Chain-nose pliers

Crimping pliers

FINISHED SIZE

20¹/₂" (52cm)

Rich purple velvet crystals in five shapes are blended together to make this sophisticated necklace. This necklace is so brilliant that it's sure to inspire tales of romance, fantasy, trickery, magic, and art—not necessarily in that order!

1 Use the 22-gauge wire to form a wrapped loop that attaches to the bar half of the clasp. String one 6mm helix bead and form a wrapped loop with a 6mm loop.

2 Use 24" (61cm) of beading wire to string 1 crimp tube, 12 size 15° seed beads, and the ring half of the clasp. Pass back through the tube and crimp.

3 For the bicone strand, string 1 galvanized size 11°, 1 crystal comet argent light 4mm, 1 galvanized size 11°, 1 purple velvet 6mm, 1 grape matte size 11°, 1 purple velvet 4mm, 1 grape matte size 11°, 1 purple velvet 6mm, 1 grape matte size 11°, 1 purple velvet 4mm, 1 galvanized size 11°, 1 crystal comet argent light 6mm, 1 galvanized size 11°, 1 purple velvet 4mm, 1 grape matte size 11°, 1 purple velvet 6mm, 1 grape matte size 11°, 1 purple velvet 4mm, 1 grape matte size 11°, and 1 purple velvet 6mm eight times. String 1 galvanized size 11°, 1 crystal comet argent light 4mm, and 1 galvanized size 11°.

4 String 1 crimp tube, 8 size 15°s, and the loop formed in Step 1. Pass back through the tube and crimp.

5 For the helix strand, repeat Step 2. String one 4mm, 1 size 15°, one 6mm, 1 size 15°, one 8mm, 1 size 15°, one 6mm, 1 size 15°, one 4mm, 1 galvanized size 11°, 1 crystal comet argent light 6mm, 1 galvanized size 11°, one 4mm, 1 size 15°, one 6mm, 1 size 15°, one 8mm, 1 size 15°, one 6mm, 1 size 15°, one 4mm, 1 galvanized size 11°, 1 crystal comet argent light 4mm, 1 size 8°, 1 crystal comet argent light 4mm, and 1 galvanized size 11° five times. String one 4mm, 1 size 15°, one 6mm, 1 size 15°, one 8mm, 1 size 15°, one 6mm, 1 size 15°, one 4mm, 1 galvanized size 11°, 1 crystal comet argent light 6mm, 1 galvanized size 11°, one 4mm, 1 size 15°, one 6mm, 1 size 15°, one 8mm, 1 size 15°, one 6mm, 1 size 15°, and one 4mm. Repeat Step 4.

6 For the rondelle strand, repeat Step 2. String one 6mm, 1 grape matte size 11°, one 8mm, 1 grape matte size 11°, one 6mm, 1 galvanized size 11°, one 6mm, 1 grape matte size 11°, one 8mm, 1 grape matte size 11°, one 6mm, 1 galvanized size 11°, 1 crystal comet argent light 6mm, 1 galvanized size 11°, one 6mm, 1 grape matte size 11°, one 8mm, 1 grape matte size 11°, one 6mm, 1 galvanized size 11°, 1 crystal comet argent light 4mm, 1 galvanized size 11°, one 8mm, 1 galvanized size 11°, 1 crystal comet argent light 4mm, and 1 galvanized size 11° seven times. String one 6mm, 1 grape matte size 11°, one 8mm, 1 grape matte size 11°, one 6mm, 1 galvanized size 11°, 1 crystal comet argent light 6mm, 1 galvanized size 11°, one 6mm, 1 grape matte size 11°, one 8mm, 1 grape matte size 11°, one 6mm, 1 galvanized size 11°, one 6mm, 1 grape matte size 11°, one 8mm, 1 grape matte size 11°, and one 6mm. Repeat Step 4.

7 For the round strand, repeat Step 2. String 1 galvanized size 11°, 1 crystal comet argent light 4mm, and 1 galvanized size 11°. *String one 6mm, 1 size 15°, one 4mm, 1 size 15°, one 8mm, 1 size 15, one 4mm, 1 size 15°, one 6mm, 1 galvanized size 11°, 1 crystal comet argent light 6mm, and 1 galvanized size 11° twice. String one 6mm, 1 size 15°, one 4mm, 1 size 15°, one 8mm, 1 size 15, one 4mm, 1 size 15°, one 6mm, 1 galvanized size 11°, 1 crystal comet argent light 4mm, 1 size 8°, 1 crystal comet argent light 4mm, and 1 galvanized size 11°. Repeat from * three times, omitting the final size 8° and crystal comet argent light 4mm. Repeat Step 4.

8 For the cube strand, repeat Step 2. *String one 8mm, 1 grape matte size 11°, one 6mm, 1 grape matte size 11°, one 8mm, 1 galvanized size 11°, 1 crystal comet argent light 6mm, and 1 galvanized size 11° twice. String one 6mm, 1 galvanized size 11°, 1 crystal comet argent light 4mm, 1 galvanized size 11°, one 8mm, 1 galvanized size 11°, 1 crystal comet argent light 4mm, 1 galvanized size 11°, one 6mm, 1 galvanized size 11°, 1 crystal comet argent light 6mm, and 1 galvanized size 11°. Repeat from * four times. String one 8mm, 1 grape matte size 11°, one 6mm, 1 grape matte size 11°, one 8mm, 1 galvanized size 11°, 1 crystal comet argent light 6mm, and 1 galvanized size 11°. String one 8mm, 1 grape matte size 11°, one 6mm, 1 grape matte size 11°, and one 8mm. Repeat Step 4.

Purely Crystal

Herkimer diamonds are named after where they were first found in Herkimer County, New York, and their diamond-like crystal structure. The stones are believed to possess strong energy and healing powers. Wear them and become open to new impressions and the surrounding world.

MATERIALS

6 rough faceted 10x18mm Herkimer
   diamond quartz crystals
5 sterling silver 10mm soldered
   jump rings
1 sterling silver 27x13mm marquis
   lobster clasp
24" (61cm) of sterling silver
   20-gauge wire

TOOLS

Wire cutters
Flat-nose pliers
Round-nose pliers
Chain-nose pliers

FINISHED SIZE

7¹/₂" (19cm)

1 Use 6" (15cm) of wire to form a double-wrapped loop that attaches to the clasp. String 1 crystal and form a wrapped loop that attaches to 1 jump ring.

2 Use 3" (8cm) of wire to form a wrapped loop that attaches to the jump ring used in the previous step. String 1 crystal and form a wrapped loop that attaches to another jump ring. Repeat three times.

3 Use 6" (15cm) of wire to form a wrapped loop that attaches to the jump ring used in the previous step. String 1 crystal and form a double-wrapped loop large enough for the clasp to attach to.

What Is a Herkimer Diamond?

What this stone isn't is a real diamond. Mined in Herkimer County, New York, this unusually beautiful clear quartz crystal is famous for its shape (it is doubly terminated or comes to a point at both ends) and for its high luster and clarity—giving it the appearance of a precious stone. Both the Mohawk Indians and early settlers in Upstate New York knew about the crystals, which they often found in stream sediments and in fields as they were cultivated. These beauties were formed nearly 500 million years ago in the Cambrian era and have been found in other parts of the world, such as Afghanistan, China, Norway, and the Ukraine. However, only those crystals found in Herkimer County are entitled to bear the name Herkimer Diamond.

Watery Origins

The word crystal derives from the Greek *krystallos,* which refers to a mythic ice palace of the Olympian gods that not even the heat of the sun could destroy. For many ancients, clear rock crystal was seen as ice suspended in rock. In China, rock crystal was also referred to as "water jade" and "thousand-year-old ice."

Herkimer diamonds

Royal Tapestry

MATERIALS

102 topaz matte size 15° seed beads (A)

176 dark gold silver-lined matte AB size 15° seed beads (B)

271 alexandrite lined size 15° seed beads (C)

72 dark purple silver-lined size 15° seed beads (D)

37 tawny topaz-lined size 11° seed beads (E)

117 amber/mauve-lined size 11° seed beads (F)

62 pale lilac AB size 11° seed beads (G)

107 purple lined size 11° seed beads (H)

40 light purple pearl frosted size 11° seed beads (I)

63 purple matte galvanized size 11° seed beads (J)

72 amber/terra-cotta-lined size 11° triangle seed beads (K)

36 shimmering rose gold-lined size 8° hex seed beads (L)

52 pale violet lined AB size 8° hex seed beads (M)

45 dark topaz 3mm cubes (N)

24 topaz 4mm crystal rounds (5000)

24 violet opal 4mm crystal rounds (5000)

36 violet 4mm crystal rounds (5000)

36 tanzanite 4mm crystal rounds (5000)

27 topaz 5.5mm crystal simplicity beads (5301)

21 violet 5.5mm crystal simplicity beads (5301)

Violet Nymo size D beading thread

TOOLS

Scissors

Thread Heaven thread conditioner

Size 12 beading needle

Thread burner

FINISHED SIZE

7" (18cm)

Many textures and colors of seed beads and crystals are brick-stitched together, causing this royal bracelet to drape like fabric around the wrist. This is the perfect piece to wear on your next magic carpet ride.

1 *Row 1:* Use a comfortable length (as long as possible) of conditioned thread and H to form a ladder stitch strip 21 beads long, leaving a 12" (31cm) tail.

Row 2: String 2N and pass the needle through the loop of thread between the second and third H in the previous row and then back through the second N just strung. Continue using brick stitch to add a total of 15N to this row.

2 Work brick stitch, adding thread as necessary, to complete the following rows.

Row 3: Add 12 units of 1C, 1 violet round, and 1C.

Row 4: Add 19F.

Row 5: Add 21J.

Row 6: Add 9 units of 1A, 1 topaz simplicity bead, and 1A.

Row 7: Add 17 units of 1B, 1M, and 1B.

Row 8: Add 20G.

Row 9: Add 24K.

Row 10: Add 12 units of 1D, 1 tanzanite round, and 1D.

Row 11: Add 20F.

Row 12: Add 12 units of 1C, 1 violet opal round, and 1C.

Row 13: Add 18 units of 1B, 1L, and 1B.

Row 14: Add 9 units of 1C, 1 violet simplicity bead, and 1C.

Row 15: Add 18E.

Row 16: Add 20I.

Row 17: Add 12 units of 1B, 1 topaz round, and 1B.

3 Repeat Rows 1–17. Repeat Rows 1–10.

Row 44: Add 20C.

4 Exit Row 44 about a quarter of the way down. String 1H, 1C, 1 violet simplicity bead, and 4C. Skip 3C and pass back through 1C, the simplicity bead, 1C, and 1H. Weave through Row 44 to exit the middle of the row. String 1H, 1C, 1 violet simplicity bead, and 4C. Skip 3C and pass back through 1C, the simplicity bead, 1C, and 1H. Weave through Row 44 to exit three-quarters of the way down. String 1H, 1C, 1 violet simplicity bead, and 4C. Skip 3C and pass back through 1C, the simplicity bead, 1C, and 1H. Stitch back through all beads just strung to reinforce, then weave in thread to secure, and trim.

5 Use the tail thread to weave through Row 1, exiting about one-quarter of the way down. String 14H (or however many will fit around the beads strung in Step 4). Skip 13H and pass back through 1H. Repeat to make a loop in the center of the row and three-quarters of the way down. Stitch back through all beads just strung to reinforce, then weave in thread to secure, and trim.

TINY GEMS:

Rock crystal beads and jewelry were common to many ancient civilizations. Treasured as a symbol of purity, rock crystal artifacts have been found in burial sites as diverse as the Mixtec site of Monte Alban in Oaxaca, Mexico, and in pre-Christian Viking graves.

Pure rock crystal is used in optical and electronic equipment, from binoculars to computers. For the timing mechanism in quartz movement watches and clocks, the crystal is likely to be synthetic. Quartz crystals have a property called the piezoelectric effect. When subjected to pressure along certain directions of the crystal, an electric voltage is produced that includes the ability to control the frequency of radio waves. Crystal is also used in polarizing microscopes because of its ability to rotate the plane of polarized light. Without this "magical" stone, we wouldn't have much of our most innovative technology, such as radar, satellite communications, cameras, televisions, and more.

Courtesy of Getty Images News

Crystals have been integral to the development of technology such as telescopes, binoculars, and microscopes. This jewel-like view of the spiral galaxy NGC 4414 was photographed by the Hubble Space Telescope.

Nouveau Riche

MATERIALS

26 amber/brick-lined size 15° seed beads

92 olivine/bronze matte metallic iris size 15° seed beads

4 crystal transparent size 11° seed beads

44 crystal matte size 11° seed beads

16 light olivine/bronze-lined AB size 11° seed beads

24 rusty orange lined size 11° seed beads

36 gold bronze metallic size 11° seed beads

15 crystal 4mm crystal bicones (5301)

16 white opal 4mm crystal bicones (5301)

12 jonquil 4mm crystal bicones (5301)

8 jonquil satin 4mm crystal bicones (5301)

28 hyacinth satin 4mm crystal bicones (5301)

6 crystal 8mm crystal top-drilled bicones (6301)

13 white opal 8mm crystal top-drilled bicones (6301)

4 jonquil 8mm crystal top-drilled bicones (6301)

1 brass 55mm princess-cut filigree

1 brass 25mm toggle clasp

2 gold-filled 2mm crimp tubes

18" (46cm) of bronze .018 beading wire

Brown Nymo size D beading thread

TOOLS

Scissors

Thread Heaven thread conditioner

Size 12 beading needle

Thread burner

Wire cutters

Crimping pliers

FINISHED SIZE

15¹/₂" (39cm)

Brass findings reminiscent of the Art Nouveau period, paired with the opalescent crystals in this necklace, are sure to make this a sought-after piece by the rich and famous. Wear this necklace in certain circles, and you'll give an entirely new meaning to the term "Nouveau Riche."

1 For the pendant, use 3' (.9m) of conditioned beading thread to string the filigree and 1 white opal 8mm bicone. Move the filigree and bead to the center of the thread. Pass back through the filigree and tie a square knot.

2 String 11 crystal matte size 11°s and pass up through the hole about ¹/₂" (1cm) from the top point of the filigree (Figure 1). String 1 white opal 8mm bicone and pass back through the filigree and size 11°s. Repeat for each point of the filigree. Use the working and tail threads to tie a square knot.

Figure 1

3 Use the tail thread to string 8 size olivine/bronze matte metallic iris size 15°s and pass up through the filigree. String 1 amber/brick-lined size 15°, 1 hyacinth satin bicone, and 2 amber/brick-lined size 15°s. Skip 1 size 15° and pass back through the size 15°, bicone, and size 15°. String 12 olivine/bronze matte metallic iris size 15°s and pass up through the filigree. String 1 olivine/bronze matte metallic iris size 15°, 1 jonquil 4mm bicone and 1 olivine/bronze matte metallic iris size 15°, and pass back through the filigree. Pass back through 12 size 15°s. String 1 size 15° and pass back through 8 size 15°s to the center of the filigree. Repeat three times around the filigree. Use both threads to tie a surgeon's knot; trim threads with the thread burner.

4 For the bail, use 12" (31cm) of conditioned beading thread to string 1 amber/brick-lined size 15° and 1 hyacinth satin bicone six times. String 1 amber/brick-lined size 15° and one loop of one point of the filigree. Pass through all beads again to form a loop. Pass through all beads again for added strength, omitting the filigree. Tie the thread ends together using a surgeon's knot. Use the thread burner to trim thread. Repeat entire step for the other loop of the same point of the filigree.

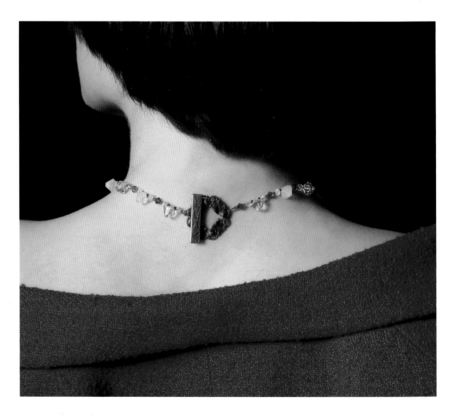

5 For the necklace, attach the beading wire to one half of the clasp using a crimp tube. String 1 rusty orange size 11°, 1 hyacinth satin bicone, 1 rusty orange, 1 crystal 4mm bicone, 1 gold bronze metallic size 11°, 1 crystal 8mm bicone, 1 gold bronze metallic, 1 crystal 4mm bicone, 1 rusty orange, 1 hyacinth satin bicone, 1 rusty orange, 1 white opal 4mm bicone, 1 gold bronze metallic, 1 white opal 8mm bicone, 1 gold bronze metallic, 1 white opal 4mm bicone, 1 light olivine/bronze lined AB size 11°, 1 jonquil satin bicone, 1 light olivine/bronze lined AB, 1 jonquil 4mm bicone, 1 gold bronze metallic, 1 jonquil 8mm bicone, 1 gold bronze metallic, 1 jonquil 4mm bicone, 1 light olivine/bronze lined AB, 1 jonquil satin bicone, 1 light olivine/bronze lined AB, 1 white opal 4mm bicone, 1 gold bronze metallic, 1 white opal 8mm bicone, 1 gold bronze metallic, and 1 white opal 4mm bicone twice. String 1 rusty orange, 1 hyacinth satin bicone, 1 rusty orange, 1 crystal 4mm bicone, 1 gold bronze metallic, 1 crystal 8mm bicone, 1 gold bronze metallic, 1 crystal 4mm bicone, 1 rusty orange, 1 hyacinth satin bicone, 1 rusty orange, 1 crystal 4mm bicone, and 1 crystal transparent size 11°.

6 String 1 loop of the bail, 1 crystal 4mm bicone, and the second loop of the bail. Repeat Step 5, reversing the stringing sequence and attaching the wire to the other half of the clasp.

did you know . . .

The Emperor's Carvings

In China, the carving of rock crystal into such objects as beads, belt hooks, figurines, funeral objects, vessels, and other utensils was a long-honored tradition, especially since the stone occurs naturally in the region. However, it wasn't until the reign of Emperor Qianlong (1736–1795) that the artistic carving of rock crystal flourished. Not only were the pieces he commissioned artistically complex and beautifully inscribed with calligraphy; they were also potentially functional. A superb collection of the pieces from this period are in a collection at the Philadelphia Museum of Art. The precision and great delicacy of these artifacts is extraordinary, especially since the crystal was most likely ground away with only bows, drills, and abrasives composed of harder minerals.

Courtesy of the Philadelphia Museum of Art: Gift of Major General and Mrs. William Crozier, 1944

This moon crystal was once in the Imperial Collection of Emperor Qianlong.

Austria's Favorite Giant

The second largest tourist attraction in this Alpine country is Swarovski's Crystal Worlds (Kristallwelten) and the giant that guards it. Created in 1995 by artist Andre Heller as an homage to the crystal company's centennial, the giant's face is both a land and water sculpture. With eyes that glow like crystals, the green giant spews forth a waterfall that drops to a pond below. The impressive guardian/greeter welcomes visitors to a cavelike museum within which a series of fantasy crystal sculptures and a three-story glass wall filled with crystals celebrate the beauty of Swarovski's vision.

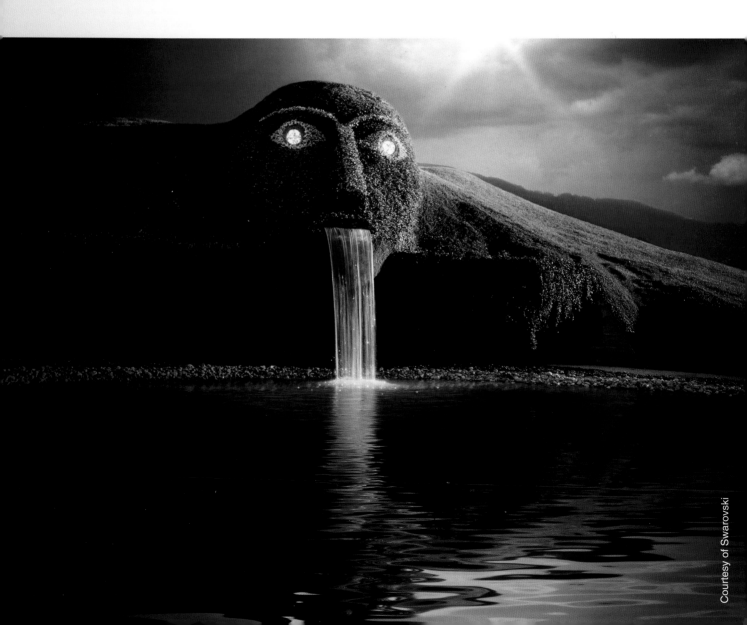

Catch a Falling Star

Dangling earrings in silver and amethyst decrease in crystal and seed bead size before exploding with an organic star shape that tickles the neck. Mix and match colors in this easy design to get different falling star effects.

MATERIALS

140 amethyst/bronze-lined AB size 15° seed beads

84 light amethyst/bronze-lined AB size 11° seed beads

50 smoky amethyst lined AB size 10° triangle seed beads

2 light amethyst AB 4mm crystal rounds (5000)

2 crystal satin 4mm crystal rounds (5000)

2 crystal satin 6mm crystal rounds (5000)

2 light amethyst 6mm crystal rounds (5000)

2 amethyst 8mm crystal rounds (5000)

2 light amethyst 20mm crystal starfish (6271)

1 pair sterling silver ear wires

Purple Nymo size D beading thread

TOOLS

Scissors

Thread Heaven thread conditioner

Size 12 beading needle

Thread burner

FINISHED SIZE

3¹/₂" (9cm)

1 Use 24" (61cm) of conditioned thread to string 9 size 15° seed beads, 1 starfish (three of the size 15°s should slide inside the starfish), and 6 size 15°s. Pass through the beads again to form a loop. Tie a square knot and trim the tail thread with the thread burner.

2 String 1 size 15°, 1 size 11°, 1 size 10°, 1 size 11°, 1 size 15°, 1 crystal satin 4mm round, 1 size 15°, 1 size 11°, 1 size 10°, 1 size 11°, 1 size 15°, 1 light amethyst 4mm round, 1 size 15°, 1 size 11°, 1 size 10°, 1 size 11°, 1 size 15°, 1 crystal satin 6mm round, 1 size 15°, 1 size 11°, 1 size 10°, 1 size 11°, 1 size 15°, 1 light amethyst 6mm round, 1 size 15°, 1 size 11°, 1 size 10°, 1 size 11°, 1 size 15°, 1 amethyst 8mm round, and 8 size 15°s. Skip 7 size 15°s and pass back through 1 size 15°, the amethyst round, and 1 size 15°.

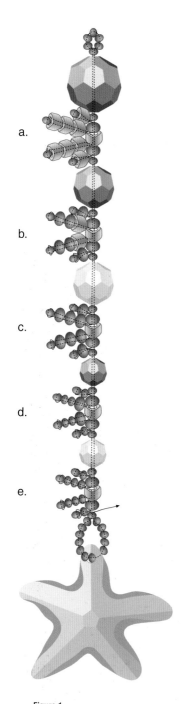

a.

b.

c.

d.

e.

Figure 1

3 String 1 size 10° and 1 size 15°. Pass back through the size 10° just strung and the size 11° on the strand. String 3 size 10°s and 1 size 15°. Pass back through the 3 size 10°s just strung and the size 10° on the strand. String 3 size 10°s and 1 size 15°. Pass back through the 3 size 10°s just strung and the size 11° on the strand. String 1 size 10° and 1 size 15°. Pass back through the size 10° and the size 15°, light amethyst 6mm round, and size 15° (Figure 1a).

4 String 1 size 11° and 1 size 15°. Pass back through the size 11° just strung and the size 11° on the strand. String 1 size 10°, 2 size 11°s, and 1 size 15°. Pass back through the 11°s and 10° just strung and the size 10° on the strand. String 1 size 10°, 2 size 11°s, and 1 size 15°. Pass back through the 11°s and 10° just strung and the size 11° on the strand. String 1 size 11° and 1 size 15°. Pass back through the size 11° and the size 15°, crystal satin 6mm round, and size 15° (Figure 1b).

5 Repeat Step 3, using size 11°s in place of size 10°s. Pass back through the size 15°, light amethyst 4mm round, and size 15° (Figure 1c).

6 Repeat Step 4, using size 11°s in place of size 10°s and size 15°s in place of size 11°s. Pass back through the size 15°, crystal satin 4mm round, and size 15° (Figure 1d).

7 Repeat Step 3, using size 15°s in place of size 10°s and passing through the loop of 15°s and the starfish (Figure 1e).

8 Pass up through the strand again, repeating Steps 7–3. Pass through the loop at the top of the earring again, then tie a knot and weave in and trim thread. Attach an ear wire to the loop at the top of the earring.

9 Repeat Steps 1–8 for a second earring.

Spring Thaw

Icy blue crystal rondelles and sterling silver accents seem to melt into spring when paired with bright green crystal bicones and leaves. The sparkly leaves in this right-angle woven necklace say spring has sprung!

MATERIALS

92 green seafoam Ceylon pearl size 15° seed beads (A)

80 green/lime-lined size 15° seed beads (B)

144 olive matte AB size 15° seed beads (C)

76 green seafoam luster size 15° seed beads (D)

76 lichen matte metallic size 15° seed beads (E)

4 teal luster size 11° seed beads (F)

4 green seafoam pearl size 11° seed beads (G)

12 citrine/lime-lined size 11° seed beads (H)

12 seafoam matte metallic iris size 11° seed beads (I)

28 Pacific opal 4mm crystal bicones (5301)

34 peridot 4mm crystal bicones (5301)

42 chrysolite 4mm crystal bicones (5301)

20 erinite 4mm crystal bicones (5301)

20 indicolite 4mm crystal bicones (5301)

18 erinite 6mm crystal rondelles (5040)

18 Pacific opal 6mm crystal rondelles (5040)

18 indicolite 6mm crystal rondelles (5040)

2 peridot 26x16mm crystal leaves (6735)

1 peridot 32x20mm crystal leaf (6735)

2 sterling silver 35x10mm leaves with crystal inlays

1 sterling silver 50x10mm hook-and-eye clasp

Green Nymo size D beading thread

TOOLS

Scissors

Thread Heaven thread conditioner

Size 13 beading needles

Thread burner

FINISHED SIZE

17¼" (44cm)

1 Use 6" (15cm) of conditioned beading thread to string 18C and one 26×16mm leaf. Pass through all beads again. Tie a surgeon's knot and use thread burner to trim threads. Repeat for the second 26×16mm leaf. Repeat, using 20C, for the 32×20mm leaf. Repeat, using 12C, for each of the sterling silver leaves. Set aside.

2 Use 8' (2m) of conditioned beading thread, with needles at both ends to string one half of the clasp. Slide the clasp to the center of the thread.

3 Use the left needle to string 1A, 1 Pacific opal bicone, 1A, 1D, 1 erinite rondelle, and 1D. Use the right needle to string 1B, 1 peridot bicone, and 1B, and pass back through the D, erinite rondelle, and D strung on the left needle (Figure 1a).

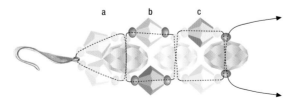

Figure 1a

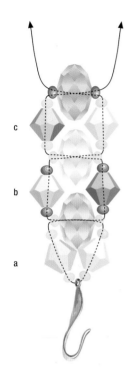

c

b

a

Figure 1b

4 Use the left needle to string 1C, 1 chrysolite bicone, 1C, 1A, 1 Pacific opal rondelle, and 1A. Use the right needle to string 1E, 1 indicolite bicone, and 1E, and pass back through the A, Pacific opal rondelle, and A strung on the left needle (Figure 1b).

5 Use the left needle to string 1D, 1 erinite bicone, 1D, 1E, 1 indicolite rondelle, and 1E. Use the right needle to string 1B, 1 peridot bicone, and 1B, and pass back through the E, indicolite rondelle, and E strung on the left needle (Figure 1c).

6 Use the left needle to string 1C, 1 chrysolite bicone, 1C, 1D, 1 erinite rondelle, and 1D. Use the right needle to string 1A, 1 Pacific opal bicone, and 1A and pass back through the D, erinite rondelle, and D strung on the left needle.

7 Use the left needle to string 1E, 1 indicolite bicone, 1E, 1A, 1 Pacific opal rondelle, and 1A. Use the right needle to string 1B, 1 peridot bicone, and 1B, and pass back through the A, Pacific opal rondelle, and A strung on the left needle.

8 Use the left needle to string 1C, 1 chrysolite bicone, 1C, 1E, 1 indicolite rondelle, and 1E. Use the right needle to string 1D, 1 erinite bicone, and 1D, and pass back through the E, indicolite rondelle, and E strung on the left needle. Repeat Steps 3-8 three times.

9 Use the left needle to string 1A, 1 Pacific opal bicone, 1A, 1C, 1 chrysolite bicone, and 1C. Use the right needle to string 1A, 1 Pacific opal bicone, and 1A, and pass back through the C, chrysolite bicone and C strung on the left needle.

10 Use the left needle to string 1I, 1D, 1 erinite rondelle, 1D, 1I, 1C, 1 chrysolite bicone, and 1C.

11 Use the right needle to string 2B, 1 peridot bicone, and 2B, and pass back through the C, chrysolite bicone, and C strung on the left needle.

12 Use the left needle to string 1E, 1 indicolite bicone, 1E, 1C, 1 chrysolite bicone, and 1C. Use the right needle to string 1D, 1 erinite bicone, and 1D, and pass back through the C, chrysolite bicone, and C strung on the left needle.

13 Use the left needle to string 1G, 1A, 1 Pacific opal rondelle, 1A, 1G, 1C, 1 chrysolite bicone, and 1C. Repeat Step 12.

14 Use the left needle to string 1D, 1 erinite bicone, 1D, 1C, 1 chrysolite bicone, and 1C. Use the right needle to string 1E, 1 indicolite bicone, and 1E, and pass back through the C, chrysolite bicone, and C strung on the left needle.

15 Use the left needle to string 1F, 1E, 1 indicolite rondelle, 1E, 1C, 1 chrysolite bicone, and 1C. Repeat Step 12.

16 Repeat Steps 10–15. Set aside.

17 Repeat Steps 1–9 using the other half of the clasp.

18 Use each needle to string 1A, 1 Pacific opal bicone, and 1A. Pass the left needle through the last C, chrysolite bicone, and C strung in Step 16. Pass the right needle back through the same three beads (Figure 2).

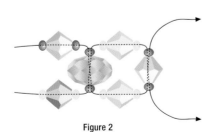

Figure 2

19 Use each needle to string 3C. Use one needle to string 1A, 1 Pacific opal bicone and 1A. Pass the other needle back through the same three beads. Use each needle to string 3C. Pass the needles, in opposite directions, through the next C, chrysolite bicone, and C (Figure 3).* Pass one needle through the E, indicolite bicone, and E and pass the other needle through the D, erinite bicone, and D, then pass the needles, in opposite directions, through the next C, chrysolite bicone, and C (Figure 4). Repeat from entire step four times, then repeat once to *.

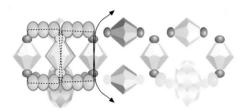

Figure 3

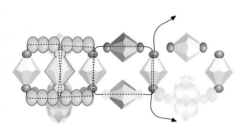

Figure 4

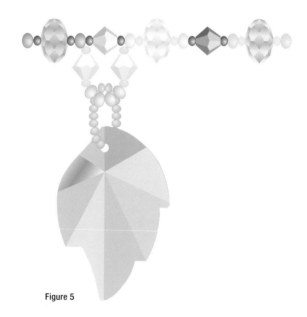

Figure 5

20 Use one needle to weave through beads exiting first E strung in Step 13. String 1C, 1 chrysolite bicone, 1C, 4H, one of the 26×16 leaf bails formed in Step 1, 1C, 1 chrysolite bicone, and 1C. Pass through the group of size 11°, size 15°, rondelle, size 15°, and size 11° (Figure 5).

21 Repeat Step 20, stringing 1B, 1 peridot bicone, 1B, 4I, 1 sterling silver leaf bail, 4I, 1B, 1 peridot bicone, and 1B.

22 Repeat Step 20, using the 30×20mm leaf. Repeat Step 21. Repeat Step 20.

23 Weave in all thread ends and trim with thread burner.

TINY GEMS:

In twelfth-century Cairo, Egypt, rock crystal beads—which had been valued at the level of diamonds—were in such great supply that they suffered price cuts.

A Rani's Paisley

This colorful embroidered brooch sparkles with crystal sew-on stones and seed beads stitched to a felt backing. You're sure to adorn yourself with this piece again and again as it is truly fit for a queen!

MATERIALS

5 g grape lined size 15° seed beads

1 g tawny topaz lined size 15° seed beads

5 g light gold bronze metallic iris size 15° seed beads

1 g light olivine gold matte silver-lined size 15° seed beads

1 g khaki purple matte metallic iris size 11° seed beads

114 bronze matte metallic iris size 8° seed beads

11 jonquil 5mm crystal sew-on stones (3128)

12 light topaz 5mm crystal sew-on stones (3128)

16 topaz 5mm crystal sew-on stones (3128)

21 tanzanite 5mm crystal sew-on stones (3128)

1 silver 1¹/₂" (4cm) pin back

3x6" (7x15cm) piece of purple felt

Piece of white paper

Purple Nymo size D beading thread

TOOLS

Pencil

Scissors

Size 10 beading needle

FINISHED SIZE

3" (7cm) diameter

1 Use the white paper and pencil to trace the design (Figure 1). The interior lines serve as guidelines and do not need to be exact. Cut all around the design just beyond the outline. Trace the cut shape onto the felt twice, cut, and set 1 piece aside.

2 Secure 6' (2m) of doubled thread to the back of the felt, passing up through it near the center of the tanzanite swirl. String 1 tanzanite sew-on stone, 1 grape size 15° seed bead, and 1 light gold bronze metallic iris size 15° seed bead. Pass back through the grape size 15°, the stone, and the felt.

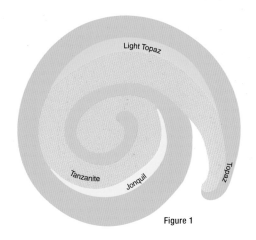

Figure 1

Pass back up through the felt and repeat, placing all the tanzanite stones and adding thread as necessary.

3 Repeat Step 2, using jonquil sew-on stones, light olivine gold matte silver-lined size 15° seed beads, and light gold bronze metallic iris size 15° seed beads.

4 Repeat Step 2, using light topaz sew-on stones, tawny topaz lined size 15° seed beads, and light gold bronze metallic iris size 15° seed beads.

5 Repeat Step 2, using topaz sew-on stones, tawny topaz lined size 15° seed beads, and light gold bronze metallic iris size 15° seed beads.

6 Fill in the large spaces between the sew-on stones by passing up through the felt and stringing 1 size 8° and 1 light gold bronze metallic iris size 15° seed bead. Pass back through the size 8° and felt. Repeat around the brooch.

7 Fill in the small spaces between the sew-on stones and the size 8° bead stacks by passing up through the felt, and string 1 size 11° seed bead and 1 grape size 15° seed bead. Pass back through the size 11° and the felt. Repeat around, using the grape size 15° seed beads around the tanzanite sew-on stones and using the light olivine gold matte silver-lined size 15° seed beads around the jonquil, light topaz, and topaz sew-on stones.

8 To make the pin back, lay your pin back in the center of the remaining piece of felt and mark the position of the hinges. Cut a small snip at each mark. Pass the pin and hinges through and close the pin so it stays in place.

9 To make the whipstitch edging, use 4' (1m) of conditioned doubled thread with a knot at the end to pass up through the back of the beaded piece of felt in the corner near the last tanzanite sew-on stone. Hold the two pieces of felt together. String 6 grape size 15°s and pass through the backing felt and beaded felt. Continue to whipstitch around the brooch, transitioning from grape size 15°s to tawny topaz lined size 15°s and to light gold bronze metallic iris size 15°s for the brooch. Tie off thread between whipstitched rows and hide the knot between beads.

special-occasion

Give the music a chance to grow on you," your friend said. And sure enough, after listening to enough recordings of popular arias by trilling sopranos, earnest tenors, and dark basso profundos, it has grown on you. You're ready for a night at the opera. You have balcony seats and your opera glasses are stashed in your beaded evening bag.

How exciting it is to contemplate dressing up for a special occasion—especially one staged in an opera house setting, where crystal chandeliers reflect the glamour and tradition of elegance behind the night's performance. Close your eyes, and it's easy to imagine horse-drawn carriages arriving, with women alighting in velvet capes and long silken gowns, wearing their richest jewels.

Your own "jewels" didn't cost a kingdom or even a small ransom. Within your jewel box of crystal confections, you've created handmade treasures worthy of any see-and-be-seen cultural event. For drama, you can wear a cocktail ring loaded with flame-red crystals that shines on your finger. Or perhaps you're leaning toward a little décolletage, graced with a daring necklace from which circles of silver and outsized crystal drops dangle. Or harkening to the Gilded Age, you choose a brilliant woven crystal lariat, silvery and regal in style.

So many options await you! Jewelry laden with gleaming crystals is its own special occasion!

Glittery Lariat

Three colors of crystals are mixed together and used at random in this sparkling right-angle weave lariat. Glass cubes at the back of the neck keep the crystal bicones from being uncomfortable. All that glitters is not gold in this fabulous lariat!

MATERIALS

10 g light sapphire bronze-lined AB size 15° seed beads

10 g blue gray matte metallic 3mm cubes

10 g silver matte metallic 3mm cubes

10 g matte metallic blue 3mm cubes

134 crystal satin 4mm crystal bicones (5301)

60 white opal satin 4mm crystal bicones (5301)

94 white opal sky blue 4mm crystal bicones (5301)

Black FireLine 6lb test

TOOLS

Scissors

Size 11 beading needle

FINISHED SIZE

27" (69cm)

1 Use a comfortable length of FireLine (as long as possible) to string 1 size 15°, 1 bicone, and 1 size 15° four times, leaving a 12" (30cm) tail. Pass through the first 3 units again (Figure 1).

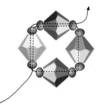

Figure 1

2 String 1 size 15°, 1 bicone, and 1 size 15° three times. Pass through the third unit strung in Step 1 and the first unit just strung (Figure 2). Repeat to work right-angle weave to form a strip 2 units wide by 15 units long.

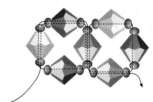

Figure 2

3 Work 2 units, randomly replacing 1 size 15°, 1 bicone, and 1 size 15° with 1 cube.

4 Work 2 units randomly replacing 2 sets of 1 size 15°, 1 bicone, and 1 size 15° with cubes.

5 Work 2 units by 42 units (10" [25cm]) of right-angle weave using cubes.

6 Repeat Step 4, then repeat Step 3.

7 Work 2 units by 17 units of right-angle weave using 1 size 15°, 1 bicone, and 1 size 15° in place of each cube.

8 String 3 size 11°s. String 1 bicone, 1 size 15°, 1 cube, and 1 size 15° eighteen times. String 1 bicone and 4 size 15°s. Skip 3 size 15°s and pass back through all beads just strung.

9 Pass through the bottom of the first unit. Repeat Step 8. Pass through the bottom of the second unit. Repeat Step 8.

10 String 3 size 11°s. String 1 cube, 1 size 15°, 1 bicone, and 1 size 15° eighteen times. String 1 bicone and 4 size 15°s. Skip 3 size 15°s and pass back through all beads just strung.

11 Pass back through the bottom of the first unit. Repeat Step 10. Pass back through the bottom of the second unit. Repeat Step 10. Weave thread to secure and trim.

12 Use the tail thread to string 1 size 15° and 1 crystal satin bicone twelve times. String 1 size 15° and pass into the strip. Pass through the first unit at the bottom of the strip. String 1 size 15° and pass through the next unit (Figure 3). Pass through all beads twice more to reinforce.

13 Weave back through the right-angle weave strip until you reach the section using cubes. Exit one cube, string 3 size 15°s, and pass through the next cube (Figure 4). Repeat for the length of the cube section of the strip, then weave through and repeat on the other side. Weave thread to secure and trim.

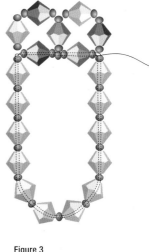

Figure 3

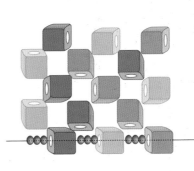

Figure 4

Cosmic Jewels

Swarovski's new cosmic crystals are the perfect starting point for these circular brick-stitch circles. Stitched together in random fashion and edged with a crystal bicone fringe, this bracelet is truly out of this world.

1 For the centerpiece, use 6' (2m) of conditioned thread to string 1 cosmic bead and pass through it twice, wrapping the thread along one side of the bead and leaving a 6" (15cm) tail. Pass through twice more so that 2 strands of thread are on each side of the beads. Pull tight and tie a square knot to stabilize the thread around the bead (Figure 1).

Round 1: String 2 olive gold matte metallic iris size 15°s; pass under the doubled thread and back through the second bead just strung. String 1 size 15°; pass under the thread and back through the size 15° (Figure 2). Repeat around, working brick stitch off the foundation thread for the circumference of the cosmic bead. Finish each round by passing down through the first bead and up through the last bead of the round.

Round 2: Work rose gold luster size 15°s all around.

Round 3: Work wintergreen opal gilt-lined size 11°s all around.

Round 4: Work rust lined AB size 11°s all around.

Figure 1

Figure 2

Round 5: Work sage silver-lined size 11°s all around.

Round 6: Work rusty orange lined size 8°s all around.

Round 7: Work sage copper-rose-magic-lined size 6°s all around. Weave in thread ends and set aside.

2 For small side pieces, repeat Step 1 using 4' (1m) of conditioned thread.

Round 1: Work rose gold luster size 15°s all around.

Round 2: Work wintergreen opal gilt-lined size 11°s all around.

Round 3: Work rusty orange lined size 8°s all around.

Round 4: Work sage copper-rose-magic-lined size 6°s all around. Set aside.

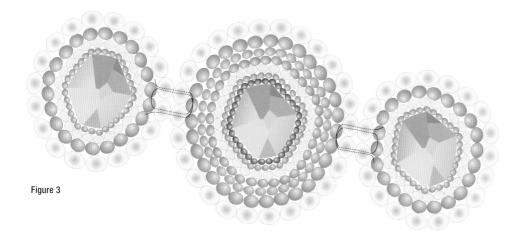

Figure 3

3 Repeat Step 2 to make a second small side piece. Use square stitch to connect the side pieces opposite each other to the centerpiece (Figure 3). Weave in tail threads.

4 For large side pieces, repeat Step 1 using 5' (2m) of conditioned thread.

Round 1: Work olive gold matte metallic iris size 15°s all around.

Round 2: Work rose gold luster size 15°s all around.

Round 3: Work sage silver-lined size 11°s all around.

Round 4: Work rusty orange lined size 8°s all around.

Round 5: Work sage copper-rose-magic-lined size 6°s all around. Set aside.

5 Repeat Step 4 to make a second large side piece. Use square stitch to connect the large side pieces to the small side pieces. Weave in tail threads.

6 For the fringe, secure 3' (1m) of conditioned thread to one of the large side pieces by weaving through several beads, exiting from a size 6° at one end of the bracelet. String 1 olive gold matte metallic iris size 15°, 1 chrysolite satin bicone, and 2 olive size 15°s. Skip 1 size 15° and pass back through 1 size 15°, the bicone, 1 size 15° and the size 6°. Pass up through the next size 6°. Repeat, using rose gold luster size 15°s and 1 crystal copper bicone. Pass back through the size 6° and up through the next size 6° and repeat using olive size 15°s and 1 chrysolite bicone. Repeat entire step around the braclet. When you reach a connection point between the pieces, string 1 size 15°, 1 bicone, and 1 size 15° and pass through a size 6° on the next piece. Weave in thread ends to secure, and trim.

7 For the edging, secure 3' (1m) of conditioned thread to 1 of the large side pieces, exiting from a size 6° at one end of the bracelet. String 3–4 olivine gold matte metallic iris size 15°s and pass down through the next size 6° and 1 size 8°. Pass up through the next size 8° and the same size 6° you just passed through. Repeat around the bracelet and pass down through the size 6° from the start of the step.

8 For the clasp, use the remaining thread from Step 7 to string 1 olive gold matte metallic iris size 15°, 5 rust lined AB size 11°s, 1 olive size 15°, 1 cosmic bead, and 4 olive size 15°s. Skip 3 size 15°s and pass back through all beads, exiting from the first rust lined size 11° string. String 1 olive size 15° and pass down through the next size 6°. Pass through all beads twice more to reinforce, then weave in thread to secure, and trim.

9 For the loop, secure 2' (.6m) of conditioned thread to the other end of the bracelet, exiting a size 6°. String 1 olive gold matte metallic iris size 15°, 5 rust lined AB size 11°, 1 olive size 15°, 1 crystal copper bicone, 1 olive size 15°, and 23 rust lined AB size 11°s. Skip 22 size 11°s and pass back through all beads into the base of the bracelet, then pass through all beads, exiting from the first rust lined size 11° strung in the loop. String 3 size olive size 15°s and pass back through 2 size 11°s. String 2 size 15°s and pass down through the third 15° strung. Pass back through 2 size 11°s and back up through the 15° (Figure 4). Repeat around the loop. Pass back through the beads connecting the loop to the bracelet, then weave in thread to secure, and trim.

Figure 4

Closeup of a magic wand hovering near the feet of actor Judy Garland, as she wears Dorothy's ruby slippers in a still from *The Wizard of Oz*.

did you know . . .

All That Glitters

Marilyn Monroe wore a glittering, skintight Jean Louis gown dripping with 6,000 Swarovski crystals when she sang "Happy Birthday" to John F. Kennedy at Madison Square Garden in 1962. This dress fetched $1.2 million at a Christie's auction in 1999. In an earlier star appearance, Swarovski crystals adorned Judy Garland's ruby red slippers in *The Wizard of Oz*. In 2000, one of the four pairs of slippers that Garland actually wore in the film was sold for $660,000.

Off with Their Jewels!

After aristocratic and royal heads rolled during the French Revolution, the upper class rushed to keep a lower profile and began to abandon their excessive displays of fine jewels. One of the humbler, less showy choices for daytime wear were rock crystal beads, which were also worn by women of the middle class.

Filigree Drops

Filigrees with a custom crystal mix called Aquadesiac were the beginning of these dangly earrings. Square-stitched circles using two different colors of crystal are linked to the filigree by yet a third crystal color, resulting in an elegant fashion statement for your ears.

MATERIALS
44 teal lined AB size 15°
 seed beads
32 teal transparent size 11°
 seed beads
16 teal matte transparent size 11°
 seed beads
48 teal lined AB size 11°
 seed beads
2 aquamarine 4mm crystal
 bicones (5301)
8 indicolite 4mm crystal bicones
 (5301)
6 blue zircon 4mm crystal bicones
 (5301)
2 aquadesiac 27mm crystal
 antique rhodium filigrees
1 pair sterling silver French wires
2 sterling silver ball head pins
12" (31cm) of sterling silver
 24-gauge wire
Teal Nymo size D beading thread

TOOLS
Scissors
Size 12 beading needle
Wire cutters
Chain-nose pliers
Round-nose pliers

FINISHED SIZE
3" (7cm)

1 Use 3' (2m) of thread to string 8 teal matte transparent size 11° seed beads. Pass through all beads again to form a circle and tie a knot, leaving an 8" (20cm) tail thread. Pass through the first bead of this round.

2 String 2 teal transparent size 11° seed beads. Pass through the last bead of the first round and through the 2 beads just strung. Repeat all around, passing through the next bead of the previous round for each 2 new beads strung (Figure 1). At the end of the round, pass through the whole round again to tighten the beads.

Figure 1

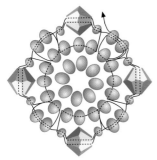

Figure 2

3 Begin the third round by stringing 2 teal lined AB size 11° seed beads and passing through the last teal transparent bead in the previous round and the two beads just strung. String 1 teal lined AB size 15° seed bead, 1 indicolite bicone, and 1 teal lined AB size 15° seed bead. Skip 2 teal transparent beads and pass back through the third teal transparent bead and the two skipped beads, then through 3 beads just strung (Figure 2). Repeat entire step all around, then pass through the whole round again.

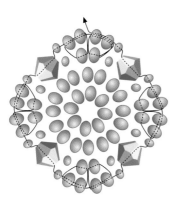

Figure 3

4 Begin the fourth round by stringing 2 teal lined AB size 11° seed beads and passing through the first size 11° in the previous round and the 2 beads just strung. String 2 teal lined AB size 11°s; pass through the next size 11° and the 2 beads just strung. String 1 size 15° and pass through the bicone in the previous round. String 1 size 15° (Figure 3). Repeat entire step all around, then pass through the whole round again. Weave in thread and trim.

5 With the tail thread exiting a bead in the first round about midway between two indicolite bicones, string 2 size 15°s, 1 aquamarine bicone, and 2 size 15°s. Pass through 1 size 11° opposite the size 11° just exited. String 1 size 15°, skip 1 size 15°, and pass back through 1 size 15°, the bicone, and 1 size 15°. String 1 size 15° and pass through the size 11° first exited. Pass through beads again to secure, then weave in thread and trim (Figure 4).

Figure 4

6 Use 1 head pin to string 1 blue zircon bicone and form a wrapped loop that attaches to the bottom of the piece just stitched.

7 Use 3" (8cm) of wire to form a wrapped loop that attaches to the top of the piece just stitched. String 1 blue zircon bicone and form a wrapped loop that attaches to 1 filigree point.

8 Use 3" (8cm) of wire to form a wrapped loop that attaches to the filigree at the point opposite the point in Step 7. String 1 blue zircon bicone and form a wrapped loop that attaches to 1 ear wire.

9 Repeat Steps 1–8 for a second earring.

The Perfect Jewel

The ancient Japanese considered rock crystal to be the "perfect jewel," symbolizing infinity, purity, patience, and perseverance. They also believed that the smaller rock crystals were the solidified breath of the White Dragon, while the larger, brighter crystals were the saliva of the Violet Dragon. Since the dragon, a cultural icon, represented the highest powers of creation, crystals were clearly held in high regard.

A Sacred Source

Not only was rock crystal used for fortune-telling and healing practices throughout history, but it was also invested with sacred status by various religions and civilizations. For Buddhists, it is one of the seven precious substances, while for the Lamas of Tibet, the eastern region of heaven is believed to be built of white crystal. Druid priests regarded crystal as a sacred power object. In the Americas, Indian medicine men used crystals as a way to communicate with the spirits. Yucatan sorcerers and Apache medicine men also used rock crystal to find lost ponies or other objects. And in Australia and New Guinea, Aborigines believe that rock crystal can help bring rain.

Courtesy of Swarovski

Toujours Topaz

MATERIALS

446 rosy topaz gold luster size 15° seed beads (A)

120 white opal 24k gold-lined size 11° seed beads (B)

12 dark copper metallic luster size 11° triangle seed beads (C)

68 dark topaz AB size 10° twisted hex seed beads (D)

96 copper-red matte metallic iris size 8° seed beads (E)

30 topaz 3mm crystal bicones (5301)

48 light Colorado topaz 3mm crystal bicones (5301)

29 burgundy 4mm crystal bicones (5301)

30 burgundy brandy 4mm crystal bicones (5301)

29 light Colorado topaz satin 5mm crystal bicones (5301)

24 light Colorado topaz 12x8mm crystal polygon beads (5203)

6 topaz 13mm crystal polygon drops (6015)

5 burgundy 21mm crystal polygon drops (6015)

25mm toggle clasp

1 sterling silver knot cup

1 gold-filled knot cup

Beige Nymo size D beading thread

TOOLS

Thread Heaven thread conditioner

Size 12 beading needle

Thread burner

FINISHED SIZE

16" (42cm)

Crystals of numerous shapes, sizes, and wonderful warm colors blend together in this luxurious netted necklace. Follow the topaz palette or decide on your own colors. Either way, this necklace is always just the right thing to wear.

1 Use 6' (2m) of conditioned thread to string the sterling silver knot cup and 1B. Tie a knot around the B, leaving an 8" (20cm) tail.

Row 1: String 1A. String 1A, 1 topaz 3mm, 1A, 1B, 1A, 1 burgundy 4mm, 1A, and 1B twenty-nine times. String 1A, 1 topaz 3mm, 2A, the gold-filled knot cup, and 1B.

2 Tie a knot around the last B strung and pass back through the knot cup and 1A.

Row 2: String 1A, 1B, 1A, 1 burgundy brandy 4mm, 1A, 1B, and 1A, and pass back through the last B strung in Row 1. String 1A, 1D, 1A, 1 light Colorado topaz satin 5mm, 1A, 1D, and 1A and pass back through the next B strung in Row 1 (Figure 1). Repeat entire step twenty-eight times.

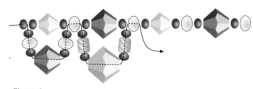

Figure 1

3 Pass through the gold-filled knot cup and 1B, then pass back through the knot cup and the beads strung in Row 1, exiting the fifth B. Pass back through the 1A, 1D, 1A, light Colorado topaz satin 5mm and 1A strung.

Row 3: String 1E, 1 light Colorado topaz 3mm, 1E, 1A, 1 polygon bead, 1A, 1E, 1 light Colorado topaz 3mm, and 1E, and pass back through the next 1A, light Colorado topaz, and 1A strung in Row 2 (Figure 2). Repeat twenty-three times.

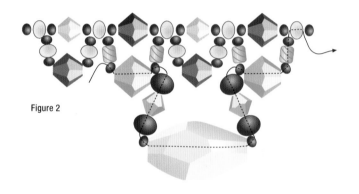

Figure 2

TINY GEMS:

On display at the Smithsonian Institution in Washington, D.C., is an enormous briolette faceted from a Brazilian rock crystal. It is in the shape of an egg and weighs 7,000 carats.

4 Pass back through the 1D and 1A from Step 2, the rest of the beads strung in Step 1, the sterling silver knot cup, and 1B. Pass back through the knot cup and beads strung in Step 1, exiting from the seventeenth B in Row 1. Pass back through beads, exiting the seventh polygon bead and 1A in Row 3.

Row 4: String 1A, 1C, 1A, 1 topaz polygon drop, 1A, 1C, and 1A, and pass back through the next 1A, polygon bead, and 1A in Row 3. String 1A, 1D, 1A, 1 burgundy polygon drop, 1A, 1D, and 1A, and pass back through the next 1A, polygon bead, and 1A in Row 3 (Figure 3). Repeat entire step five times. String 1A, 1C, 1A, 1 topaz polygon drop, 1A, 1C, and 1A, and pass back through the next 1A, polygon bead, and 1A in Row 3. Pass back through all beads back to Row 1, then pass back through all beads in Row 1, the gold-filled knot cup, and the 1B.

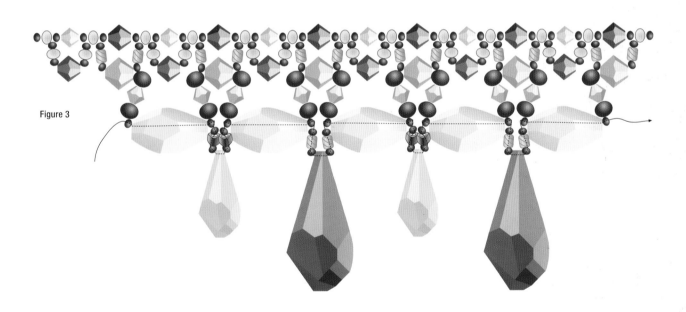

Figure 3

5 Tie a knot around the 1B. Pass back through beads and tie knots to secure, then trim thread. Repeat with tail thread.

6 Attach the sterling silver knot cup to ring half of the clasp. Attach the gold-filled knot cup to the bar half of the clasp.

A Crystal-lode

In 1719, a group of crystal hunters (*cristalliers*) were prospecting in Zinggenstock, Switzerland. In a granitic massif, the hunters found a huge cavity, more than 30 feet long, filled with quartz. The vein ultimately produced more than 50 tons of crystals, the largest of which weighed almost 900 pounds. It boggles the mind to imagine how such giant crystals were transported in those times!

You Say Essex, I Say Wessex

In England in the mid- to late-nineteenth century, intricately carved and crafted rock crystal cabochons, called Essex crystals or reverse crystals, or even Wessex crystals, were the fashion. Motifs for the carvings were often animals, both wild and sporting. Skilled artists painstakingly carved the rock crystal out from the back then painted the depressions in detail. The largest and most detailed of these crystal cabochons, when viewed from the side, appear lifelike in their three-dimensionality. Because these carved crystals were extremely skill- and labor-intensive, the technique died out by the early twentieth century.

Courtesy of Georgian Jewelry, www.georgianjewelry.com

The horse and hound motifs were common in Essex crystals.

Ring of Fire

Sharp points of bicone crystals and spiky fringe explode from a metal screen ring base, making this one hot cocktail ring. Wear this to your next party and watch out as everyone stands back from the heat exuding from your ring of fire!

MATERIALS

42 amethyst gold luster size 15° seed beads (A)

57 garnet gold luster size 15° seed beads (B)

63 raspberry lined AB size 15° seed beads (C)

27 olive opaque luster size 15° seed beads (D)

27 champagne lined size 15° seed beads (E)

39 smoky topaz transparent size 15° seed beads (F)

14 rose satin 4mm crystal bicones (5301)

19 ruby 4mm crystal bicones (5301)

21 ruby satin 4mm crystal bicones (5301)

9 khaki 4mm crystal bicones (5301)

9 light smoked topaz 4mm crystal bicones (5301)

13 smoked topaz 4mm crystal bicones (5301)

1 antique brass 22x30mm screen ring

Dark pink Nymo size D beading thread

TOOLS

Scissors

Thread Heaven thread conditioner

Size 12 beading needle

Thread burner

FINISHED SIZE

1 1/2" diameter (4cm)

1 Thread the needle to the center of 8' (2m) of conditioned thread. Use both ends of thread to tie a double overhand knot.

2 Pass up through the center of the screen. Mentally divide the screen into six pie pieces and stitch one slice/color at a time (Figure 1).

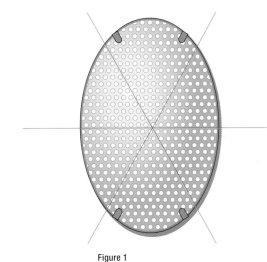

Figure 1

3 String 1C, 1 ruby satin bicone, and 2C. Skip 1C and pass back through 3 beads and the screen. Pass up through the screen and repeat. Repeat to fill an entire slice with ruby satin bicones.

4 Skip a slice and repeat Step 3 using B and ruby bicones.

5 Skip a slice and repeat Step 3 using A and rose satin bicones.

6 Repeat Step 3 using F and smoked topaz bicones to fill the slice between the ruby and rose satin bicones.

7 Repeat Step 3 using E and light smoked topaz bicones to fill the slice between the ruby and ruby satin bicones.

8 Repeat Step 3 using D and khaki bicones to fill the remaining slice.

Crystals in Camelot

With its shimmering wireworked crystal and silver pendant, this necklace brings to mind leisurely days in Camelot. You're sure to dream of many new legends of hope and romance when you wear it. Perhaps even a handsome prince will ride in on a white horse.

MATERIALS

32 red copper metallic size 11° seed beads

42 maroon 6mm crystal pearl rounds

23 crystal moonlight 2mm crystal rounds (5000)

9 crystal moonlight 3mm crystal rounds (5000)

20 crystal moonlight 6mm crystal rondelles (5040)

10 vintage rose 8mm crystal cubes (5601)

3 crystal moonlight 20mm crystal cosmic pendants (6680)

1 sterling silver 17mm VeeO Vogue ring

4 sterling silver 21mm VeeO Vogue rings

2 sterling silver 2mm crimp tubes

2 sterling silver 3mm crimp covers

1 sterling silver 8mm soldered jump ring

2 sterling silver 26mm head pins

34" (86cm) of sterling silver 22-gauge wire

19" (48cm) of silver satin .015 beading wire

TOOLS

Wire cutters

Crimping pliers

Flat-nose pliers

Round-nose pliers

Crimping pliers

FINISHED SIZE

16½" (42cm)

1 Use 2" (5cm) of wire to wrap two 21mm rings together. Make five complete wraps around the rings, which will overlap, then trim wire ends behind the rings. Repeat to attach all four rings.

2 Use 3" (8cm) of wire to wrap three complete wraps around the top of the left ring in the middle row. String 1 rondelle, 1 cube, and 1 rondelle, and wrap the wire three times around the connection of this ring with the bottom ring. Repeat for the right ring in the middle row.

3 Use 4" (10cm) of wire to form a wrapped loop that attaches to 1 cosmic pendant. String 1 pearl and one 3mm round. Hold the wire just above the 3mm round to the bottom of the ring on the right in the middle row. Wrap the wire around the ring two and one half times. Repeat entire step for the other ring in the middle row.

4 Use 5" (13cm) of wire to form a wrapped loop that attaches to 1 cosmic pendant. String 1 pearl and one 3mm round. Hold the wire just above the 3mm round to the bottom of the bottom ring. Wrap the wire around the ring two and one half times, then cross the wire over the back of the wraps and wrap twice more on the opposite side of the center wire. String 1 rondelle, 1 cube, and 1 rondelle, and wrap the wire two and one half times around the top of this ring.

5 Use 4" (10cm) of wire to wrap the bottom half of the top ring two and one half times. String 1 rondelle, 1 cube, and 1 rondelle. Wrap the wire around the top of the ring twice. String one 3mm round, 1 pearl, and one 3mm round. Hold the wire just above the 3mm round to the bottom of the 17mm ring. Wrap the wire around the ring two and one half times, then cross the wire over the back of the wraps and wrap twice more on the opposite side of the center wire.

6 Use 1 head pin to string one 3mm round and form a wrapped loop. Repeat with the other head pin. Use 3" (8cm) of wire to form a wrapped loop that attaches to 1 head pin loop. String one 3mm round, 1 pearl, the soldered jump ring, and one 3mm round and form a wrapped loop that attaches to the other head pin loop.

7 Attach the beading wire to the jump ring using a crimp tube. Cover the tube with a crimp cover. String 1 size 11°, 1 pearl, 1 size 11°, 1 cube, 1 size 11°, and 1 rondelle three times. String 1 size 11°, 1 pearl, 1 size 11°, and 1 rondelle three times. String 1 size 11°. String 1 pearl and one 2mm round twenty-three times. String 1 pearl, 1 size 11°, 1 rondelle, and 1 size 11° four times. String 1 cube, 1 size 11°, 1 pearl, 1 size 11°, 1 rondelle, and 1 size 11° twice. String 1 cube, 1 size 11°, 1 pearl, 1 size 11°, 1 crimp tube, and the 17mm ring. Pass back through the tube; crimp and cover.

Courtesy of Getty Images/AFP Staff

Indian jewelry trader G.P. Gupta displays the world's largest transparent and colorless crystal ball, 28cm in diameter and weighing 29kg, which was made from a 450kg rough stone mined from Nepal, at the annual international jewelry trade show in Tokyo in January 2007. The crystal ball has an estimated price of 500 million yen (4.2 million USD), Gupta said.

In a Crystal Ball

Need to foretell the future or get advice for a difficult decision? A crystal ball was just the thing for clairvoyants in the Middle Ages (A.D. 500 to 1500). Early crystal balls were made entirely of carved and polished rock crystal. Also called "crystallomancy" or "scrying," crystal gazing is known as the art of concentrating on a crystal ball in order to achieve a psychic state in which divination can be accomplished. This glassy oracle was often used by kings and conquerors of old who looked deeply within for revelation about a conquest's outcome or the progress of more personal matters. Picture the Wicked Witch of the West viewing Dorothy's journeys in Oz in her crystal ball and you have a vision of how fantasy stories have also depended on crystal gazing.

As for who made the best seers, either prepubescent boys or young virgins were believed to be the most apt. Widows took third place. "Charging" was an important aspect of the process of crystal gazing in which one imbued the crystal with purity, magnetism, and spiritual qualities. For this, dark-eyed, dark-skinned brunettes were believed to charge the crystal more quickly because of their "magnetic" temperament. Another step in preparing the crystal sphere was to place it in a grave for at least three weeks.

Because of the expense and rarity of stones large enough to produce pure rock crystal balls, modern versions of the diviner's tool are more likely to be made of leaded glass, acrylics, or even Plexiglas.

"The Skull of Doom"

It was said to be a pre-Columbian crystal skull, found beneath the altar of a Mayan temple. And best of all, it was full of wild possibilities. It was the relic of a lost civilization. It was crafted by extraterrestrials or wizards. It held supernatural powers. According to F.A. Mitchell-Hedges, a British banker and adventurer, and his daughter, Anna (who "discovered" it in Belize in the 1920s), the skull had been made 3,600 years ago and could cause misfortune and death. At least these were the stories with which the pair enthralled an interested public.

Although none were ever excavated, a number of similar crystal skulls found their way into museum collections around the world. The Smithsonian National Museum of Natural History received the donation of such a skull in 1992. At the venerable institution, researchers used a high-tech microscope to expose the hoax of these skulls. What they could see upon close examination was that the skulls had been carved with modern coated lapidary wheels using industrial diamonds. So much for the antiquity and the mystical powers of these crystal artifacts.

Daniel Swarovski, Crystal Innovator

Since the eighteenth century, the glassmakers in Bohemia have been renowned for their precision gem cutting. After studying in Paris, young Daniel Swarovski returned to Bohemia to become a gem cutter in his father's business. Eventually, he developed a reputation for producing small, high-quality, brilliant-cut glass crystals. Because of the high demand in Europe and America for his faceted crystals, in 1892 Swarovski developed and patented a machine that cut crystals faster and with greater precision than could be done manually.

Daniel Swarovski, founder of the Swarovski crystal empire. The crystal innovator stands next to his patented crystal faceting machine.

To keep his valuable and revolutionary invention under wraps, in 1895 he moved his family to Wattens, Austria, a small village near Innsbruck. Here he found the seclusion, abundant natural water power, and dedicated workers that helped him nurture the now-$2 billion industry Swarovski has become.

Like most business successes, technological ingenuity and innovation wasn't the only thing at which the company excelled. Over the decades, the founder and his heirs have proven themselves masterful market strategists. For example, Swarovski has, since the mid-twentieth century, worked closely with influential fashion designers—notably Coco Chanel and Elsa Schiaparelli—to incorporate crystals in their clothing and accessories. Later fans included Christian Dior, Gianni Versace, Yves St. Laurent, Dolce & Gabbana, and Roberto Cavalli. Today, the company's crystals are runway regulars.

The Healing Powers of Crystal

Long before today's New Age believers appropriated rock crystal as a healing force, the ancient Egyptians, Babylonians, and Assyrians believed that placing crystals on various parts of the body brought healing energy to wounds and illnesses. In medieval Europe, rock crystal was used to treat a number of ailments. The stone was ground into a powder and mixed with wine to remedy such diverse problems as dysentery, gout, and colic. The Romans held pieces of crystal against the tongue to reduce fevers. In his writings, Roman scholar Pliny the Elder (A.D. 23–79) described how a crystal ball could concentrate sunlight in order to cauterize wounds. And in the Scottish Highlands, crystal stones were believed to cure hydrophobia, take away diseases of horned cattle, and counteract infections.

fashion-forward

Each year you look forward to your city's independent film festival. You love the cinema, and this is your chance to be among the first to weigh in on the year's worthiest new efforts. Best of all, these films haven't been buried in hype yet. No wonder you feel a little like a film critic: your vote counts.

So many films, so many tickets, so many nights out. Think of the opportunities you'll have to wear your most fashion-conscious jewelry—artfully made by you, of course. Showy bangles studded with bright crystals and wrapped in a crystal mesh are a fabulous accessory. They feel just right as you gesture and talk in the theater lobby with friends who share your passion for film and fashion.

Or how about espresso and dessert at a nearby coffeehouse, where you show off your necklace of silver and rock crystal chunks? If a visiting director walked in right now, you'd look like a star. You can also exude drama in your dark layered necklace of crystal, crystal pearls, and crystal crosses. Express your inner diva with the styles in this section of the book. By "diva," we mean the artistic you who revels in playing with and setting trends by wearing jewelry with attitude. Crystals are especially suited to this effort. It's showtime!

Brilliant Bangles

MATERIALS

56 silvery gray lined size 15° seed beads (A)

96 seafoam AB size 15° seed beads (B)

96 pink champagne lined size 15° seed beads (C)

96 soft olivine gold luster size 15° seed beads (D)

1 g shadow crystal opal gilt-lined size 11° seed beads (E)

10 g pale aqua lined size 11° seed beads (F)

10 g peach lined AB size 11° seed beads (G)

10 g light olivine bronze-lined size 11° seed beads (H)

44 light azore 4mm crystal bicones (5301)

44 silk 4mm crystal bicones (5301)

44 khaki 4mm crystal bicones (5301)

8 crystal silver shade 5mm crystal bicones (5301)

20 crystal silver shade 6mm crystal bicones (5301)

13 light azore 6mm crystal bicones (5301)

13 silk 6mm crystal bicones (5301)

13 khaki 6mm crystal bicones (5301)

3 silver 8mm magnetic clasps

Gray Nymo size D beading thread

TOOLS

Scissors

Thread Heaven thread conditioner

Size 12 beading needles

Thread burner

FINISHED SIZE

7¹/₂" (19cm)

Three tubular herringbone tubes are accented with sparkling crystals, the placements of which give the tubes the appearance of being twisted. The magnetic clasps of each tube are hidden under a band of right-angle weave crystals that tie this pastel palette together. Brilliant!

1 Use 8' (2m) of conditioned thread to ladder-stitch 8F, leaving a 10" (25cm) tail. Pass through the first and last beads to form a tube, exiting from the top of the first bead.

2 String 2F. Pass down through the next bead and up through the following bead in the previous round. Repeat three more times. Step up by passing up through the first bead strung in this round.

3 Repeat Step 2 for a total of six rounds.

Figure 1

4 String 1B, 1 light azore 4mm bicone, 1B, and 3F. Pass down through the next bead and up through the following bead in the previous round. String 2F. Pass down through the next bead and up through the following bead in the previous round (Figure 1). Repeat entire step to finish the round. Step up by passing up through the B, bicone, and B, down through 3F, and up through the next 1F.

5 String 2F. Pass down through the next bead and up through the following bead in the previous round. Repeat from the beginning of this step. String 2F. Pass down through the next bead, up through the B, bicone, and B, down through 3F, and up through the next 1F. Repeat entire step to finish the round. Step up by passing up through the B, bicone, and B, down through 23F, and up through the next 1F (Figure 2). Repeat entire step to complete a third round in this manner.

Figure 2

6 String 2F. Work herringbone around the tube, passing through the unit of B, bicone, and B when necessary (Figure 3).

7 Repeat Step 2 (Figure 4).

Figure 3

8 Repeat Steps 4–7 thirty-nine times, moving the crystal over one column each time to give the appearance of a crystal spiral.

9 Repeat Step 2 for a total of six rounds.

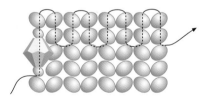

Figure 4

10 String 3B and one half of 1 clasp. Pass down through the F opposite of the one just exited and up through the following bead. Pass through the B and clasp again to reinforce, then weave thread through beads to secure and trim. Repeat, using the tail thread, on the other end of the tube with the other half of the clasp.

11 Repeat Steps 1–10 using G, C, silk 4mm bicones, and a second clasp.

12 Repeat Steps 1–10 using H, D, khaki 4mm bicones, and the third clasp.

13 Use 5' (1.5m) of conditioned thread to string 1D, 1 khaki 6mm bicone, and 1D four times. Pass through the first three groups of three beads.

14 String 1D, 1 khaki 6mm bicone, and 1D three times. Pass through the third group of three beads in the previous unit and the first two groups of this unit.

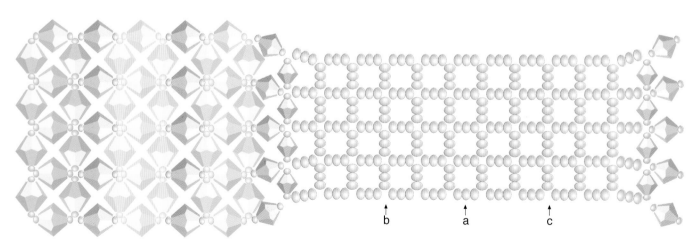

Figure 5

15 Continue working right-angle weave for a total of four khaki units. Follow the illustration (Figure 5) to work a strip of right-angle weave, blending colors and eventually switching to 5mm bicones, then size 11° seed beads. Work eleven units (four units wide) of right-angle weave using size 11° seed beads. Switch back to 5mm bicones, then 6mm bicones.

16 Use 2' (.6m) of conditioned thread to stitch the peach tube to the center of the strip formed in Step 15 (Figure 5a). Weave through the strip and attach the blue tube to the strip (Figure 5b), then weave through to the other side of the peach strip and attach the green tube (Figure 5c).

17 Use right-angle weave to stitch the two ends of the strip together, with the tubes on the inside. Weave in thread to secure, and trim.

TINY GEMS:
Ladies in fashionable ancient Roman society carried crystal balls in their hands to cool themselves during the heat of summer.

Ruby Dreams

MATERIALS

10 g garnet matte silver-lined size 15° seed
beads

175 salmon rose silver-lined size 11° seed
beads

8 padparadscha 3mm crystal bicones (5301)

8 Indian red 3mm crystal bicones (5301)

8 Siam 3mm crystal bicones (5301)

8 turquoise 3mm crystal bicones (5301)

2 turquoise 4mm crystal bicones (5301)

1 padparadscha 18x13mm crystal fancy
stone (4120)

1 Indian red 18x13mm crystal fancy stone
(4120)

1 Siam 18x13mm crystal fancy stone
(4120)

1 sterling silver 13x19mm loop d' loop hook-
and-eye clasp

4 sterling silver 2x3mm crimp tubes

40" (102cm) of .014 beading wire

Red Nymo size D beading thread

TOOLS

Scissors

Thread Heaven thread conditioner

Size 12 beading needles

Size 15 beading needle

Wire cutters

Bead stops

Crimping pliers

FINISHED SIZE

16½" (42cm)

Three fancy stones in subtly different shades of red
are secured with seed bead bezels and connected
with turquoise bicones. Two thin strands of tiny seed
beads and crystals are all that's needed to showcase this striking pendant.

1 For the bezels, use 8' (2m) of conditioned beading thread and
size 15° seed beads to form a right-angle weave strip that fits
snuggly around the widest point of the padparadscha fancy
stone, leaving a 12" (31cm) tail thread. Connect the ends of the
strip and fit the stone inside. Use the tail thread to work one row
of peyote stitch around the front of the stone to tighten the strip
and secure the stone. Work peyote stitch around the back of the
stone, decreasing to tighten the beads, caging the stone in place,
until the entire back of the stone is covered (see below).

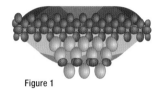

Figure 1

2 Weave back through beads to one of the long sides of the stone. From the original right-angle weave strip, work peyote stitch to attach 5 size 11° seed beads to the center of the stone (Figure 1). Work a second row of peyote to attach 4 size 11° seed beads. Work a third row of peyote, stringing 1 size 15°, 1 size 11°, and 1 size 15° between each size 11° of the previous row. Work back through beads to exit the middle size 11° of this row. Set aside.

3 Repeat Steps 1 and 2 using the Siam fancy stone. Repeat Step 1 using the Indian red fancy stone. Repeat Step 2 on both long sides of the Indian red stone.

4 To connect the bezels, use the working thread of the padparadscha stone to string 1 size 15°, 1 turquoise 4mm bicone, and 1 size 15°. Pass through the middle size 11° of the Indian red bezel and back through the 15°, bicone, and 15°. Weave back through size 15°s in the bezel to secure, and trim thread. Use the working thread of the Indian red stone to pass back through the 15°, bicone, and 15°. Pass through the middle size 11° of the padparadscha bezel and through the 15°, bicone, and 15°. Weave back through size 15°s in the bezel to secure, and trim thread. Repeat to attach the other side of the Indian red bezel to the Siam bezel, but do not trim thread on the Siam bezel.

5 To make the bail, use the thread on the Siam bezel to weave through size 15°s to the other long size of the stone. From the original right-angle weave strip, work peyote stitch to attach 5 size 11° seed beads to the center of the stone. Work a peyote string 9 rows long and 7 beads wide. Connect the first and last beads to form a bezel. Weave back through beads to secure thread and trim.

6 To make the necklace, cut the beading wire in half. Attach both wires to one half of the clasp using a crimp tube.

7 Use one wire to string 1 size 11°, 1 size 15°, 1 turquoise 3mm, 1 size 15°, 1 size 11°, 15 size 15°s, 1 size 11°, 1 size 15°, 1 Siam bicone, 1 size 15°, 1 size 11°, 15 size 15°s, 1 size 11°, 1 size 15°, 1 Indian red bicone, 1 size 15°, 1 size 11°, 15 size 15°s, 1 size 11°, 1 size 15°, 1 padparadscha bicone, 1 size 15°, and 1 size 11° twice.

8 String 40 size 15°s and the pendant. Repeat Step 7, reversing the sequence.

9 Repeat Steps 7–8 using the other wire, and switching the placement of the Siam and padparascha bicones.

10 Use both wires to string 1 crimp tube and the other half of the clasp. Pass back through the tube and crimp.

Medieval Mood

MATERIALS

68 olive opaque luster size 15° seed beads
73 grape silver-lined size 15° seed beads
54 silver size 11° seed beads
32 olivine 4mm crystal bicones (5301)
32 amethyst 4mm crystal bicones (5301)
9 olivine satin 5mm crystal bicones (5301)
27 amethyst 5mm crystal rounds (5000)
3 amethyst 20mm crystal crosses (6866)
6 light green 5mm crystal pearls (5810)
8 mauve 5mm crystal pearls (5810)
4 dark green 5mm crystal pearls (5810)
10 light green 8mm crystal pearls (5810)
6 mauve 8mm crystal pearls (5810)
10 dark green 8mm crystal pearls (5810)
10 light green 10mm crystal pearls (5810)
10 mauve 10mm crystal pearls (5810)
10 dark green 10mm crystal pearls (5810)
6 sterling silver 2mm crimp tubes
Sterling silver toggle clasp
60" (152cm) of .019 beading wire
24" (61cm) Nymo size D beading thread

TOOLS

Scissors
Thread Heaven thread conditioner
Size 12 beading needle
Thread burner
Wire cutters
Crimping pliers

FINISHED SIZE

16" (41cm)

Three strands of pearls and crystals in royal purple and green shine like an artifact from ages past. The classic square cross shape of the crystal pendants is reminiscent of Medieval castles, churches, and knights in shining armor. To round out the mood of this piece, the cross shape is repeated in the sterling toggle clasp.

1 Use 8" (20cm) of conditioned beading thread to string 1 amethyst crystal round and 1 grape silver-lined size 15° four times. String 1 cross and 5 size 15°s. Pass through all beads again to form a circle. Pass through all beads again and form a surgeon's knot. Use a thread burner to trim thread. Repeat for a total of three cross dangles. Set aside.

2 Attach 19" (48cm) of beading wire to one half of the clasp, using a crimp tube. String 1 olive size 15°. String 1 light green 5mm pearl, 1 silver size 11°, 1 amethyst round, 1 size 11°, 1 dark green 5mm pearl, 1 olive size 15°, 1 olivine bicone, 1 olive size 15°, 1 mauve 8mm pearl, 1 olive size 15°, and 1 olivine bicone twice. String 1 olive size 15°, 1 light green 5mm pearl, 1 silver size 11°, 1 amethyst round, 1 silver size 11°, 1 dark green 8mm pearl, 1 olive size 15°, 1 olivine bicone, 1 olive size 15°, 1 mauve 8mm pearl, 1 olive size 15°, 1 olivine bicone, 1 olive size 15°, 1 light green 8mm round, and 1 silver size 11°. String 1 amethyst round, 1 silver size 11°, 1 dark green 10mm pearl, 1 olive size 15°, 1 olivine bicone, 1 olive size 15°, 1 mauve 10mm pearl, 1 olive size 15°, 1 olivine bicone, 1 olive size 15°, 1 light green 10mm round, and 1 silver size 11°.

3 String 1 amethyst round. Repeat Step 2, reversing the sequence and attaching the beading wire to the other side of the clasp.

4 Attach 20" (51cm) of beading wire to one half of the clasp using a crimp tube. String 1 silver size 11°, 1 olivine satin bicone, 1 silver size 11°, 1 amethyst bicone, and 1 grape size 15°. String 1 light green 8mm pearl, 1 grape size 15°, 1 amethyst bicone, 1 grape size 15°, 1 mauve 5mm pearl, 1 grape size 15°, 1 amethyst bicone, 1 grape size 15°, 1 dark green 8mm pearl, 1 grape size 15°, 1 amethyst bicone, 1 silver size 11°, 1 olivine satin bicone, 1 silver size 11°, 1 amethyst bicone, and 1 grape size 15° eight times, omitting the final amethyst bicone and grape size 15°. String 1 crimp tube and the other half of the clasp. Pass back through the tube and crimp.

5 Attach 21" (53cm) of beading wire to one half of the clasp using a crimp tube. String 1 silver size 11°, 1 amethyst round, 1 silver size 11°, 1 light green 10mm pearl, 1 olive size 15°, 1 olivine bicone, 1 olive size 11°, 1 mauve 10mm pearl, 1 olive size 11°, 1 olivine bicone, 1 olive size 15°, and 1 dark green 10mm pearl three times. String 1 silver size 11°, 2 grape size 15°s, 1 cross dangle from Step 1, 1 silver size 11°, 1 light green 10mm pearl, 1 olive size 15°, 1 olivine bicone, 1 olive size 15°, 1 mauve 10mm pearl, 1 olive size 15°, 1 olivine bicone, 1 olive size 15°, 1 dark green 10mm pearl, 1 silver size 11°, and 1 grape size 15°.

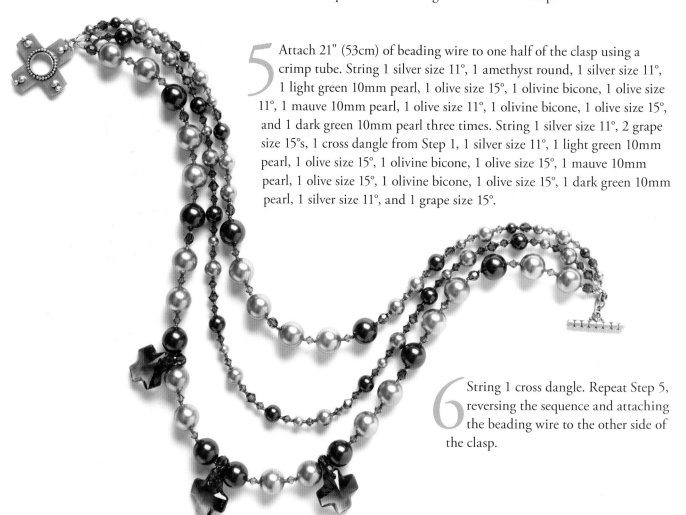

6 String 1 cross dangle. Repeat Step 5, reversing the sequence and attaching the beading wire to the other side of the clasp.

did you know . . .

The Rock

Performer Liberace's passion for over-the-top sparkle was legendary. In addition to his many shimmering costumes, he owned a Baldwin piano encrusted with Swarovski crystals. In 1982, in recognition of the entertainer's penchant for crystals, Swarovski presented him with an enormous 51-pound, 115,000-carat crystal.

Pianist Liberace, the original "Bling King." Note the glittering piano, one of the pianist's signature possessions.

Blue-Green Reflections

MATERIALS

147 soft olivine gold luster size 15° seed beads

147 olive olivine-lined size 15° seed beads

147 deep turquoise opaque luster size 15° seed beads

4 gold bronze matte size 15° seed beads

8 light olivine bronze-lined size 11° seed beads

8 olive olivine-lined size 11° seed beads

8 teal peacock-lined size 11° seed beads

22 gold bronze size 11° seed beads

10 lime 6mm crystal rounds (5000)

10 khaki 6mm crystal rounds (5000)

10 Caribbean blue opal 6mm crystal rounds (5000)

8 crystal dorado 2X 6mm crystal rounds (5000)

3 crystal dorado 2X 20mm crystal square rings (4439)

Dark brown Nymo size D beading thread

TOOLS

Scissors

Thread Heaven thread conditioner

Size 12 beading needle

Thread burner

FINISHED SIZE

8" (20cm)

Strands of blue and green crystals and seed beads attach to three crystal rings of silver and gold. The crystal rings are each the same color. The middle ring is reversed to display the gold back while the two end rings display the silver side. The result is a shimmering, reflective delight.

1 Use 18" (15cm) of thread to string 20 deep turquoise size 15° seed beads and 1 square ring. Pass through all beads again to form a loop and tie a square knot. String 1 deep turquoise size 15°, 1 crystal dorado 2X round, 21 deep turquoise size 15°s, and a second square ring. Pass through the last 20 size 15°s just strung again to form a loop, then pass back through the size 15°, the round, and 1 size 15°. Use the tail and working threads to tie a surgeon's knot. Use the thread burner to trim thread.

2 Repeat Step 1 to attach the third square ring.

3 Repeat Steps 1 and 2 using soft olivine gold luster size 15° seed beads. Repeat again using olive olivine-lined size 15° seed beads, placing the connections on the opposite side of the deep turquoise connections as the soft olivine gold luster.

4 Use 30" (76cm) of thread to string 3 deep turquoise size 15°s, leaving a 6" (15cm) tail. String 1 Caribbean blue opal round, 1 deep turquoise size 15°, 1 teal peacock-lined size 11°, and 1 deep turquoise size 15° four times. String 1 Caribbean blue opal round, 21 deep turquoise size 15°s and 1 square ring. Pass through the last 20 size 15°s strung to form a loop. Pass back through all beads strung.

5 String 17 gold bronze size 11°s. Skip 16 and pass back through the first gold bronze size 11° strung.

6 Use thread to repeat Step 4, using soft olivine gold luster size 15° seed beads, light olivine bronze-lined size 11° seed beads, and lime crystal rounds. Pass through all beads in Step 5.

7 Use thread to repeat Step 4, on the other side of the blue beads, using olive olivine-lined size 15° seed beads, olive olivine-lined size 11° seed beads, and khaki crystal rounds. Pass through all beads in Step 5. Tie a surgeon's knot, weave thread through beads to secure, and trim.

8 Repeat Step 4 for the other side of the bracelet.

9 String 1 gold bronze size 11°, 1 gold bronze matte size 15°, 1 crystal dorado 2X round, and 1 gold bronze matte size 15° twice. String 3 gold bronze size 11°s. Skip two size 11°s and pass back through all beads.

10 Repeat Step 6, passing through and back through all beads in Step 9. Repeat Step 7, passing through and back through all beads in Step 9. Tie a surgeon's knot, weave thread through beads to secure, and trim.

TINY GEMS:

At its factory in Wattens, Austria, the Swarovski company produces a billion crystals each week.

Mystic Crystal

In the Middle Ages, some people believed that gods and spirits lived in palaces made from rock crystal. Others believed rock crystal could quench thirst. To keep the focus on this powerful crystal, this necklace is simply strung with silver beads.

MATERIALS
36 russet metallic galvanized size 11°
 seed beads
18 rough faceted 16mm rock crystal rounds
17 Thai silver 8x18–16x18mm shaped beads
1 sterling silver 35mm toggle clasp
2 sterling silver 3mm crimp tubes
21" (53cm) of sterling silver .024 beading wire

TOOLS
Wire cutters
Crimping pliers

FINISHED SIZE
18³/₄" (48cm)

1 Attach the wire to one half of the clasp using a crimp tube.

2 String 1 seed bead, 1 quartz crystal, 1 seed bead, and 1 Thai silver bead. Repeat sixteen times.

3 String 1 seed bead, 1 quartz crystal, 1 seed bead, 1 crimp tube, and the other half of the clasp. Pass back through the tube and crimp.

Lush Layers

MATERIALS

14 crystal brandy 4mm crystal rounds (5000)

8 crystal chili 4mm crystal rounds (5000)

36 rose brandy 4mm crystal bicones (5301)

20 aqua brandy 4mm crystal bicones (5301)

8 Pacific opal brandy 4mm crystal bicones (5301)

19 aqua champagne 4mm crystal bicones (5301)

15 aqua champagne 5mm crystal bicones (5301)

13 aqua champagne 6mm crystal bicones (5301)

10 crystal chili 8mm crystal rondelles (5040)

4 crystal brandy 12mm crystal cosmic beads (5523)

4 crystal brandy 11x10mm crystal flat pear briolettes (6012)

4 crystal chili 11x10mm crystal flat pear briolettes (6012)

6 light rose champagne 11x10mm crystal flat pear briolettes (6012)

8 aqua champagne 11x10mm crystal flat pear briolettes (6012)

66 sterling silver 2mm cornerless cubes

1 sterling silver 5-strand tube clasp

10 sterling silver 2mm crimp tubes

50" (127cm) of .019 beading wire

TOOLS

Wire cutters

Crimping pliers

FINISHED SIZE

7¼" (18cm)

Five simply strung strands of crystals feel exotic and opulent against your skin. Due in part to special color coatings, such as brandy and champagne, the crystals in this bracelet will sparkle and shine like no others.

1 Attach 10" (25cm) of beading wire to the first loop of one half of the clasp using a crimp tube. String 1 cornerless cube and 1 Pacific opal brandy bicone. String 1 cornerless cube, 1 cosmic bead, 1 cornerless cube, 1 crystal chili round, 1 cornerless cube, 1 crystal chili round, 1 cornerless cube, 1 crystal brandy briolette, 1 cornerless cube, 1 Pacific opal brandy bicone, 1 cornerless cube, and 1 Pacific opal brandy bicone four times, omitting the final cornerless cube and Pacific opal brandy bicone. String 1 crimp tube and the first loop of the other half of the clasp. Pass back through the tube and crimp.

2 Attach 10" (25cm) of beading wire to the second loop of one half of the clasp using a crimp tube. String 1 aqua champagne 5mm bicone and 1 rose brandy bicone twice. String 1 cornerless cube, 1 aqua champagne briolette, and 1 cornerless cube. String 1 rose brandy bicone and 1 aqua champagne 5mm bicone four times. String 1 rose brandy bicone, 1 cornerless cube, 1 aqua champagne briolette, and 1 cornerless cube. String 1 rose brandy bicone and 1 aqua champagne 5mm bicone three times. String 1 rose brandy bicone, 1 cornerless cube, 1 aqua champagne briolette. String 1 rose brandy bicone and 1 aqua champagne 5mm bicone four times. String 1 rose brandy bicone, 1 cornerless cube, 1 aqua champagne briolette, and 1 cornerless cube. String 1 rose brandy bicone and 1 aqua champagne 5mm bicone twice. String 1 crimp tube and the second loop of the other half of the clasp. Pass back through the tube and crimp.

3 Attach 10" (25cm) of beading wire to the third loop of one half of the clasp. String 1 crystal brandy round and 1 aqua champagne 4mm bicone twice. String 1 cornerless cube, 1 light rose champagne briolette, 1 cornerless cube, 1 aqua champagne 4mm bicone, 1 crystal brandy round, 1 aqua champagne 4mm bicone, 1 crystal brandy round, and 1 aqua champagne 4mm bicone six times, omitting the final aqua champagne bicone. String 1 crimp tube and the third loop of the other half of the clasp. Pass back through the tube and crimp.

4 Attach 10" (25cm) of beading wire to the fourth loop of one half of the clasp. String 1 rose brandy bicone, 1 aqua champagne 6mm bicone, 1 rose brandy bicone, 1 aqua champagne 6mm bicone, 1 rose brandy bicone, 1 cornerless cube, 1 aqua champagne briolette, and 1 cornerless cube. String 1 rose brandy bicone, 1 aqua champagne 6mm bicone, 1 rose brandy bicone, 1 aqua champagne 6mm bicone, 1 rose brandy bicone, 1 aqua champagne 6mm bicone, 1 rose brandy bicone, 1 cornerless cube, 1 aqua champagne briolette, and 1 cornerless cube three times. String 1 rose brandy bicone, 1 aqua champagne 6mm bicone, 1 rose brandy bicone, 1 aqua champagne 6mm bicone, 1 rose brandy bicone, 1 crimp tube, and the fourth loop of the other half of the clasp. Pass back through the tube and crimp.

5 Attach 10" (25cm) of beading wire to the fifth loop of one half of the clasp. String 1 aqua brandy bicone, 1 rondelle, 1 aqua brandy bicone, 1 cornerless cube, 1 aqua brandy bicone, 1 rondelle, 1 aqua brandy bicone, 1 cornerless cube, 1 crystal chili briolette, and 1 cornerless cube five times, omitting the final cornerless cube, briolette, and cornerless cube. String 1 crimp tube and the fifth loop of the other half of the clasp. Pass back through the tube and crimp.

In Support of the King

After the execution of England's King Charles I in 1649, many loyal followers of the Stuart monarch began to wear memorial rings in his honor. The rings often had a faceted rock crystal, which was set atop locks of the king's hair, his initials, or a likeness of the doomed fated king. This style of commemorative jewelry became known as Stuart Crystal Jewelry and remained a popular fashion until the mid-eighteenth century.

Ravenscroft—Inventor or Entrepreneur?

An Englishman named George Ravenscroft is often credited with originating the formula for leaded glass, a formula still remarkably close to the one used today. He did patent the formula and technique in the late-seventeenth century. But many scholars and glass aficionados now dispute his claim. Lead oxide (the material used as a flux in creating leaded glass) was already being used in Italy to produce paste jewelry at the time of Ravenscroft's discovery. Plus, the Englishman had strong links with the Venetian glass environment (he lived in Venice for fifteen years). Additionally, the enterprising Ravenscroft was engaged by an English glass company to advance research on glassmaking. To do this, Ravenscroft hired Italian glassmakers—most prominent among them, Giacomo da Costa. There is little doubt that da Costa gave Ravenscroft the formula for lead crystal, which he soon patented.

Courtesy of Georgian Jewelry, www.georgianjewelry.com

These two examples of Stuart crystal jewelry were worn by Charles I loyalists in the seventeenth century.

Azure Treasure

The romantic nature of this simple necklace is achieved with the blending of indicolite crystals and vintage-looking brass findings. The result is a magical treasure.

MATERIALS

280 aqua/Montana-lined AB size 15°
    seed beads
9 jet nut 2X 4mm crystal bicones (5301)
23 indicolite satin 4mm crystal bicones
    (5301)
10 indicolite 4mm crystal bicones (5301)
8 indicolite satin 6mm crystal rondelles
    (5040)
9 indicolite 20mm crystal avant-garde
    pendants (6620)
8 brass 4x20mm links
4 brass 12x18mm 2-to-1 connectors
1 brass 20mm toggle clasp
5 brass 6mm jump rings
14 brass 2" (5cm) head pins
32" (81cm) of 4mm brass ladder chain
40" (102cm) black FireLine 6lb test

TOOLS

Scissors
Size 13 beading needle
Wire cutters
Flat-nose pliers
Chain-nose pliers
Round-nose pliers

FINISHED SIZE

18" (46cm)

1 Cut the chain into one $15^1/_2$" (39cm) piece and one $16^1/_2$" (42cm) piece.

2 Cut the flat end off of each head pin.

3 Hold two 2-to-1 connectors back to back. Use 1 jump ring to attach the connectors to the ring half of the clasp.

4 Use 1 head pin to form a simple loop that attaches to the bar end of the toggle. String 1 indicolite satin bicone and form a simple loop that attaches to the two remaining connectors.

5 Use jump rings to attach the chains to the connectors.

6 Use a surgeon's knot to tie the FireLine to one end of the $15^1/_2$" (39cm) chain, leaving an 8" (20cm) tail. String 20 seed beads and pass up through the second link of chain and down through the fourth link.

7 String 1 indicolite satin bicone and 10 seed beads and pass up through the sixth link of chain. String 1 indicolite bicone and 10 seed beads and pass down through the eighth link of chain. String 1 jet nut 2X bicone and 10 seed beads and pass up through the tenth link of chain. String 1 rondelle and 10 seed beads and pass down through the twelfth link of chain. Repeat entire step eight times, passing up/down through every other link of chain, and omitting the final rondelle. String 10 seed beads and tie the thread to the final link of chain. Weave thread ends back through the strand, tying square knots every 1/2" (1cm) or so.

8 Use 1 head pin to form a simple loop that attaches to 1 pendant. String 1 indicolite satin bicone and form a simple loop. Repeat for a total of 5 pendant dangles.

9 Use 1 head pin to form a simple loop that attaches to 1 pendant. String 1 indicolite satin bicone and form a simple loop that attaches to 2 links held back to back. Use 1 head pin to form a simple loop that attaches to the other end of the links. String 1 indicolite bicone and form a simple loop. Repeat for a total of 4 pendant-link dangles.

10 Attach 1 pendant dangle to the center of the 16½" (42cm) chain. *Skip 2 links and attach 1 pendant-link dangle. Skip two links and attach 1 pendant dangle. Skip 2 links and attach 1 pendant-link dangle. Skip 2 links and attach 1 pendant dangle. Repeat from * on the other side of the center pendant dangle.

techniques and findings

TECHNIQUES

Crimping

Crimp tubes are seamless tubes of metal that come in several sizes. To use, string a crimp tube through the connection finding. Pass back through the tube, leaving a short tail. Use the back notch of the crimping pliers to press the length of the tube down between the wires, enclosing them in separate chambers of the crescent shape. Rotate the tube 90° and use the front notch of the pliers to fold the two chambers onto themselves, forming a clean cylinder. Trim the excess wire.

Crimp covers hide a crimp tube and give a professional finish. To attach, gently hold a crimp cover in the front notch of the crimping pliers. Insert the crimped tube and gently squeeze the pliers, encasing the tube inside the cover.

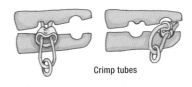

Crimp tubes

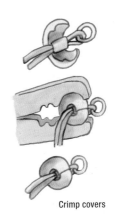

Crimp covers

Finishing and Starting New Threads

Tie off your old thread when it's about 4" (10cm) long by making a simple knot between beads. Pass through a few beads and pull tight to hide the knot. Weave through a few more beads and trim the thread close to the work. Start the new thread by tying a knot between beads and weaving through a few beads. Pull tight to hide the knot. Weave through several beads until you reach the place to resume beading.

Knots

Half Hitch Knot

Half hitch knots may be worked with two or more strands—one strand is knotted over one or more other strands. Form a loop around the cord(s). Pull the end through the loop just formed and pull tight. Repeat for the length of cord you want to cover.

Half hitch knot

Lark's Head Knot

Lark's head knots are great for securing stringing material to another piece, such as a ring or a donut. Begin by folding the stringing material in half. Pass the fold through a ring or donut. Pull the ends through the loop created and pull tight.

Lark's head knot

Overhand knot

Square knot

Surgeon's knot

Overhand Knot

The overhand knot is the basic knot for tying off thread. Make a loop with the stringing material. Pass the cord that lies behind the loop over the front cord and through the loop. Pull tight.

Square Knot

The square knot is the classic sturdy knot for securing most stringing materials. First make an overhand knot, passing the right end over the left end. Next, make another overhand knot, this time passing the left end over the right end. Pull tight.

Surgeon's Knot

The surgeon's knot is very secure and therefore good for finishing off most stringing materials. Tie an overhand knot, right over left, but instead of one twist over the left cord, make at least two. Tie another overhand knot, left over right, and pull tight.

Pass Through vs Pass Back Through

"Pass through" means to move your needle in the same direction that the beads have been strung. "Pass back through" means to move your needle in the opposite direction.

Stitches

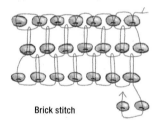

Brick stitch

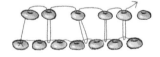

Brick stitch decrease

Brick Stitch

Begin by creating a foundation row in ladder stitch or using a secured thread. String 2 beads and pass under the closest exposed loop of the foundation row and back through the second bead. String 1 bead and pass under the next exposed loop and back through the bead just strung; repeat.

To decrease within a row, string 1 bead and skip a loop of thread on the previous row, passing under the second loop and back through the bead.

To increase within a row, work two stitches in the same loop on the previous row.

Ladder Stitch

Using two needles, one threaded on each end of the thread, pass one needle through 1 or more beads from left to right and pass the other needle through the same beads from right to left. Continue adding beads by crisscrossing both needles through 1 bead at a time. Use this stitch to make strings of beads or as the foundation for brick stitch.

For a single-needle ladder, string 2 beads and pass through them again. String 1 bead. Pass through the last stitched bead and the one just strung. Repeat, adding 1 bead at a time and working in a figure-eight pattern.

Ladder stitch (double needle)

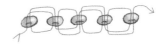

Ladder stitch (single needle)

Right-Angle Weave (Single Needle)

String 4 beads and pass through them again to form the first unit. For the rest of the row, string 3 beads, pass through the last bead passed through in the previous unit, and the first two just strung; the thread path will resemble a figure eight, alternating directions with each unit. To begin the next row, pass through the last 3 beads strung to exit the side of the last unit. String 3 beads, pass through the last bead passed through, and the first bead just strung. *String 2 beads, pass through the next edge bead of the previous row, the last bead passed through in the previous unit, and the last 2 beads just strung. Pass through the next edge bead of the previous row, string 2 beads, pass through the last bead of the previous unit, the edge bead just passed through, and the first bead just strung. Repeat from * to complete the row, then begin a new row as before.

To make a row-end decrease, weave thread through the second bead added in the second-to-last group from the previous row. Begin the new row by stringing 3 beads. Pass back through the first bead added in the second-to-last group from the previous row. Pass through the beads just added. Continue across the row, adding two beads at a time.

To make a row-end increase, begin a new row as usual, exiting thread from the third bead just added. String 3 beads. Pass back through the third bead added in the last set (making a figure eight). Weave to the first bead added in this set and continue across the row, adding 2 beads at a time.

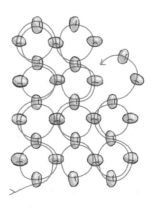

Right-angle weave (single needle)

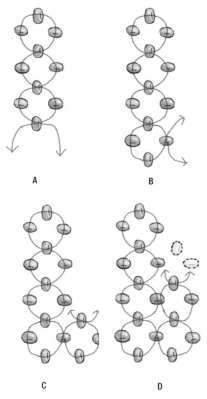

A B

C D

Right-angle weave (double needle)

Right-Angle Weave (Double Needle)

Using one needle on each end of the thread, string 3 beads to the center of the thread.*Use one needle to string 1 bead, then pass the other needle back through it. String 1 bead on each needle, then repeat from * to form a chain of right-angle units (A).

To turn at the end of the row, use the left needle to string 3 beads, then cross the right needle back through the last bead strung (B). Use the right needle to string 3 beads, then cross the left needle back through the last bead strung (C). To continue the row, use the right needle to string 2 beads; pass the left needle through the next bead on the previous row and back through the last bead strung (D).

Peyote Stitch

One-drop peyote stitch begins by stringing an even number of beads to create the first two rows. Begin the third row by stringing 1 bead and passing through the second-to-last bead of the previous rows. String another bead and pass through the fourth-to-last bead of the previous rows. Continue adding 1 bead at a time, passing over every other bead of the previous rows. Two-drop peyote stitch is worked the same as above, but with 2 beads at a time instead of 1.

To make a mid-project decrease, simply pass thread through 2 beads without adding a bead in the "gap." In the next row, work a regular one-drop peyote over the decrease. Keep tension taut to avoid holes.

To make a mid-project increase, work a two-drop over a one-drop in one row. In the next row, work a one-drop peyote between the two-drop. For a smooth increase, use very narrow beads for both the two-drop and the one-drop between.

Zipping or zipping up a piece of flat peyote stitch entails folding the beadwork so the first and last rows match. The beads should interlock like a zipper. (If the beads don't interlock, add or subtract one row from the beadwork.) Pass through 1 bead of the first row and the next bead of the last row, lacing the beads together, to create a seamless tube.

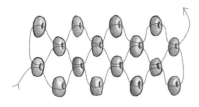

One-drop peyote stitch

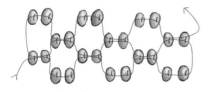

Two-drop peyote stitch

Square Stitch

Begin by stringing a row of beads. For the second row, string 2 beads, pass through the second-to-last bead of the first row, and back through the second bead of those just strung. Continue by stringing 1 bead, passing through the third-to-last bead of the first row, and back through the bead just strung. Repeat this looping technique to the end of the row.

To make a decrease, weave thread through the previous row and exit from the bead adjacent to the place you want to decrease. Continue working in square stitch.

To make an increase, string the number of beads at the end of the row you want to increase. Work the next row the same as the previous row.

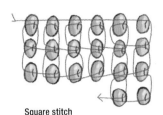

Square stitch

Tubular Herringbone Stitch

Begin with a foundation row of ladder stitch. Join the ends together to form a tube. String 2 beads. Pass down through the next bead and up through the bead after it. Repeat around the tube. At the end of the round, pass through the first beads of the previous and current rounds to step up to the new round.

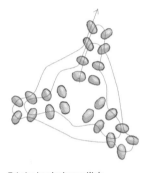

Tubular herringbone stitch

Simple Fringe

Exit from your foundation row of beads or fabric. String a length of beads plus 1 bead. Skipping the last bead, pass back through all the beads just strung to create a fringe leg. Pass back into the foundation row or fabric.

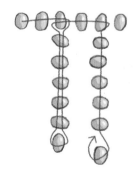

Simple fringe

Stringing

Stringing is a technique in which you use a beading wire, needle and thread, or other material to gather beads into a strand.

Stringing

Tension bead

Tension Bead

String a bead larger than those you are working with, then pass through the bead one or more times, making sure not to split your thread. The bead will be able to slide along but will still provide tension to work against when you're beading the first two rows.

Wireworking

Simple loop

To form a simple loop, use flat-nose pliers to make a 90° bend at least ½" (1cm) from the end of the wire. Use round-nose pliers to grasp the wire after the bend; roll the pliers toward the bend, but not past it, to preserve the 90° bend. Use your thumb to continue the wrap around the nose of the pliers. Trim the wire next to the bend. Open a simple loop by grasping each side of its opening with a pair of pliers. Don't pull apart. Instead, twist in opposite directions so that you can open and close without distorting the shape.

To form a wrapped loop, begin with a 90° bend at least 2" (5cm) from the end of the wire. Use round-nose pliers to form a simple loop with a tail overlapping the bend. Wrap the tail tightly down the neck of the wire to create a couple of coils. Trim the excess wire to finish. Make a thicker, heavier-looking wrapped loop by wrapping the wire back up over the coils, toward the loop, and trimming at the loop.

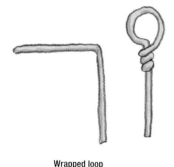

Wrapped loop

PROJECT RESOURCES

Materials

Arabian Nights, 18
Seed beads: Beyond Beadery
Clasp: Kate McKinnon

Azure Treasure, 112
Seed beads and Swarovski crystal rondelles: Beyond Beadery
Brass findings: Vintaj Natural Brass Findings: Fusion Beads

Blue-Green Reflections, 102
Seed beads: Beyond Beadery

Brilliant Bangles, 88
Seed beads: Beyond Beadery
Magnetic clasps: Hobby Lobby

Catch a Falling Start, 38
Seed beads: Beyond Beadery
Ear wires: Fusion beads

Cosmic Jewels, 58
Seed beads: Beyond Beadery

Crystals in Camelot, 80
VeeO Vogue rings: Via Murano
Beading wire: Beadalon
Seed beads: Beyond Beadery

Filigree Drops, 64
Filigree and ear wires: Fusion Beads
Seed beads: Bead Cache

Glittery Lariat, 54
Seed beads: Beyond Beadery

Lush Layers, 108
Swarovski crystals: Beyond Beadery
Cornerless cubes: Saki Silver
Clasp: Fusion Beads

Medieval Mood, 98
Seed beads: Beyond Beadery
Clasp: Rishashay

Mystic Crystal, 106
Seed beads: Beyond Beadery
Quartz crystals: Soft Flex Company
Thai silver and toggle clasp: Saki Silver

Nouveau Riche, 32
Seed beads: Beyond Beadery
Vintaj natural brass filigree and clasp: Fusion Beads

Purely Crystal, 22
Crystal: Soft Flex Company
Clasp: Fusion Beads
Jump rings: The Bead Goes On

Ring of Fire, 76
Screen ring: Ornamentea
Seed beads: Beyond Beadery

A Rani's Paisley, 48
Pin back and felt: Jo-Ann
Seed beads: Beyond Beadery

Royal Tapestry, 26
Seed beads: Beyond Beadery

Ruby Dreams, 94
Clasp: Fusion Beads
Seed beads: Beyond Beadery

Spring Thaw, 42
Sterling silver leaves: Jill MacKay
Clasp: Somerset Silver
Seed beads: Beyond Beadery

Toujours Topaz, 70
Clasp: Saki Silver
Seed beads: Beyond Beadery

Sources

Beyond Beadery
PO Box 460
Rollinsville, CO 80474
(800) 840-5548
www.beyondbeadery.com

Bead Cache
3307 S. College, Ste. 105
Fort Collins, CO 80525
(970) 224-4322

Beadalon
440 Highlands Blvd.
Coatesville, PA 19320
(866) 4BEADALON (423-2325)
www.beadalon.com

The Bead Goes On
PO Box 592, 14 Church St.
Vineyard Haven
Martha's Vineyard, MA 02568
(866) 861-2323
www.beadgoeson.com

Fusion Beads
3830 Stone Wy. North
Seattle, WA 98103
(888) 781-3559
www.fusionbeads.com

Hobby Lobby
www.hobbylobby.com

Jill MacKay
www.jillmackay.com

Jo-Ann
www.joann.com

Kate McKinnon
www.katemckinnon.com

Ornamentea
509 N. West St.
Raleigh, NC 27603
(919) 834-6260
www.ornamentea.com

Rishashay
PO Box 8271
Missoula, MT 59807
(800) 517-3311
www.rishashay.com

Saki Silver
362 Ludlow Ave.
Cincinnati, OH 45220
(513) 861-9626
www.sakisilver.com

Soft Flex Company
PO Box 80
Sonoma, CA 95476
(866) 925-FLEX (3539)
www.softflexcompany.com

Somerset Silver
PO Box 253
Mukilteo, WA 98275
(425) 641-3666
www.somerset-silver.com

Via Murano
17654 Newhope St., Ste. A
Fountain Valley, CA 92708
(877) VIAMURANO

Vintaj Natural Brass Findings
PO Box 246
Galena, IL 61036
www.vintaj.com

For more beading designs and techniques, join the community at beadingdaily.com where life meets beading or subscribe to Interweave's beading magazines:

Beadwork

Step by Step Beads

Step by Step Wire Jewelry

Stringing

INDEX